BOWLS
of Glory

◆

FIELDS
of Dreams

School spirit is sky high at this University of Tennessee football game at Neyland Stadium in Knoxville. Courtesy, University of Tennessee, Knoxville

Produced in cooperation with the Stadium Managers Association

Cherbo Publishing Group, Inc. Encino, California

BOWLS *of Glory* ◆ FIELDS *of Dreams*

GREAT STADIUMS and BALLPARKS of NORTH AMERICA

by Steve Blickstein

CHERBO PUBLISHING GROUP, INC.
PRESIDENT JACK C. CHERBO · VICE PRESIDENT
ELAINE HOFFMAN · EDITORIAL DIRECTOR KAREN STORY
PRODUCTION DIRECTOR JAMES BURKE · ACQUISITIONS/SALES
COORDINATOR J.J. HANSEN · ADMINISTRATIVE COORDINATOR JOAN BAKER
STAFF FOR *BOWLS OF GLORY, FIELDS OF DREAMS*
SENIOR EDITOR TERI DAVIS GREENBERG · CORPORATE PROFILE
EDITOR KAREN L. O'ROURKE · EDITORIAL ASSISTANT
KATHY B. PEYSER · DESIGNER ELLEN IFRAH · REGIONAL
MANAGER MARCIA WEISS · PUBLISHER'S
REPRESENTATIVE STEVE NAFE

©1995 BY CHERBO PUBLISHING
GROUP, INC. ALL RIGHTS
RESERVED. PUBLISHED 1995.
LIBRARY OF CONGRESS CATALOG
CARD NUMBER: 95-69779
ISBN: 1-882933-05-2

PHOTOS COURTESY (CLOCKWISE FROM TOP LEFT): ARAMARK CORP.; CPG ARCHIVES;
THE CLEVELAND BROWNS; JAMES BLANK / SCENICS OF AMERICA; HOK SPORTS FACILITIES
GROUP

Contents

*A*cknowledgments

If the author learned anything writing *Bowls of Glory, Fields of Dreams*, it's that there's a lot to learn about stadiums. I'd like to take this opportunity to thank a number of individuals, groups, and institutions for their time and generosity in making that learning experience easier and, in some cases, pleasurable.

Starting at the drawing board with the architects who patiently guided me through the intricacies of stadium design: special thanks to Jerry Anderson and Bob Fatovic of Anderson DeBartolo Pan, Rick deFlon of Ellerbe Becket, Ron Labinski and Dennis Wellner of HOK Sports Facilities Group, Terry Miller of Howard Needles Tammen and Bergendoff (HNTB) and Dale Swearingen of Osborn Engineering.

I can't find enough words to thank the stadium managers, too numerous to mention here, who not only revealed and explained the complexities of running a stadium, but also put me in touch with other invaluable sources of information. They have a demanding job, and they do it with consummate professionalism.

My appreciation to the following for spending hours sharing their inexhaustible knowledge of stadiums and sports with me: my very good friends—public relations mogul Joe Epley, Jr., baseball memorabilia meister Peter Keyser, and sports trivia maven extraordinaire John C. Smith; Bob Zeig and Andy Deitel of the Brooklyn Sports Foundation; sports marketing consultant Max Muhleman; and Jim Steeg of the National Football League.

For sharing their archives and memories, I am grateful to Robert Daley, who trusted me with the collected works of his father, Arthur Daley of the *New York Times* and the greatest sports writer who ever lived; Sue Schmid, editor and publisher of *Athletic Business* magazine; and Joe Laurice and Marty Adler, keepers of the flame of the Brooklyn Dodgers, the Dodger Hall of Fame, and the Brooklyn Dodger Symphony. Into this same category falls Philip Lowry and his deservedly acclaimed *Green Cathedrals*. Less well-known, but equally valuable, is Lowry's *Green Gridirons*, a historical tour of the NFL's playing fields.

I not only thank, but also applaud, NFL veterans Bobby Bell, Len Dawson, the dynamic broadcasting duo of Sam Huff and Sonny Jurgensen, Robert Jackson, Greg Pruitt, and Jan Stenerud for recalling their stadium experiences so candidly and amusingly.

I'd be remiss if I did not mention the sports information departments of a host of colleges and universities, the capable and responsive public relations staffs in pro football and major-league baseball, and the baseball and pro football halls of fame.

Most of all, I thank my loving and supportive wife Jennie, to whom I dedicate this book.

Steve Blickstein
May 1995

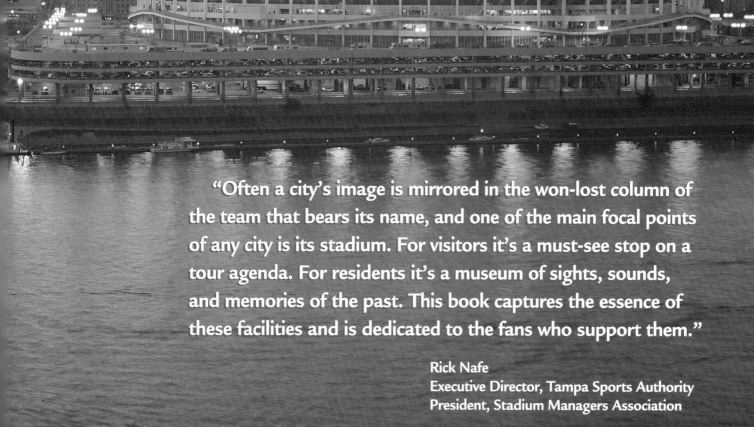

"Often a city's image is mirrored in the won-lost column of the team that bears its name, and one of the main focal points of any city is its stadium. For visitors it's a must-see stop on a tour agenda. For residents it's a museum of sights, sounds, and memories of the past. This book captures the essence of these facilities and is dedicated to the fans who support them."

Rick Nafe
Executive Director, Tampa Sports Authority
President, Stadium Managers Association

An illuminated Riverfront Stadium joins the city of Cincinnati at twilight. Photo by James Blank / Scenics of America

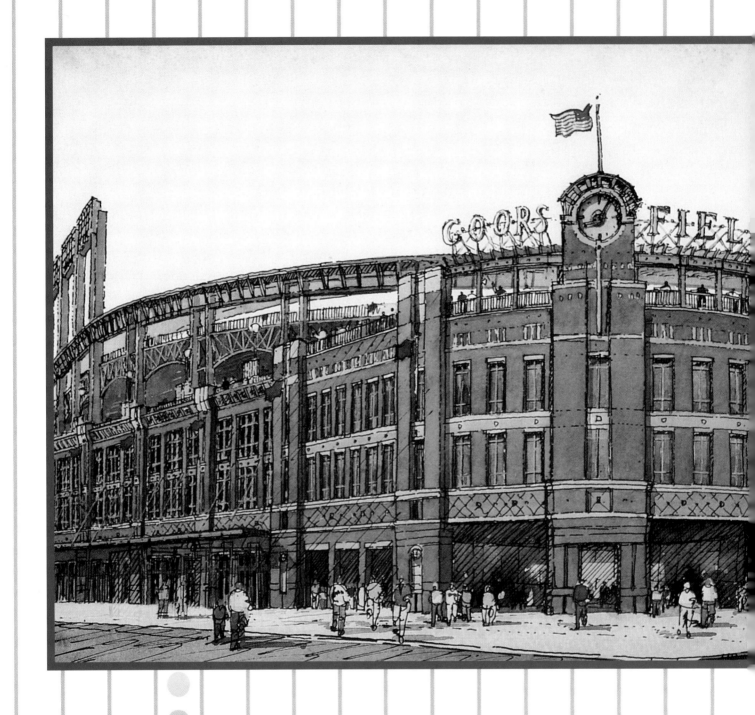

*C*oors Field, Denver's baseball-only stadium, appeals to fan nostalgia with its resemblance to ballparks of bygone days. Courtesy, HOK Sports Facilities Group

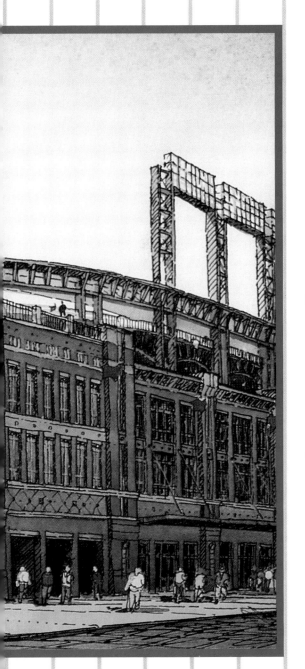

THE EVOLUTION OF STADIUMS

Work in Progress

Ever since the ancient Greeks sat on crudely terraced dirt embankments to watch their athletes run the first known measured foot races, stadiums have been theaters of sports and spectacles. Today millions of spectators a day flock to North America's premier stadiums and ballparks to witness a wondrous variety of big-time sports and spectacular attractions in conditions that range from merely comfortable to luxurious.

From the centuries before Christ until today, the mission of the stadium—to provide a field for players and seats for spectators—hasn't changed. What has changed is the manner in which this mission is accomplished. Today's stadiums and ballparks are entering a brave new world of elaborately constructed, technologically advanced, all-weather, fan-friendly, multipurpose event environments. Here are just a few examples of the changes in progress:

• Start with long-standing amenities—Souvenir stands that once sold only pennants and pins have evolved into specialty retail shops. Hot dog concessions are being transformed into food courts. Tip-cadging ushers have metamorphosed into neatly dressed, courteous hosts trained in crowd control and, in some cases, cardiopulmonary resuscitation.

• Thanks to the introduction of alcohol-free family sections and supervised playgrounds for children, spectators no longer need to worry about being exposed to foul-mouthed, beered-up fans.

• The scoreboard, once content to show numbers of balls and strikes or yards to go for a first down, is now an excursion into virtual

Though originally built in about 600 B.C., the Roman Circus Maximus measured nearly 1,850 feet long and 280 feet wide and could seat about 200,000 spectators after Julius Caesar had it reconstructed and enlarged in 319 B.C. This early stadium was primarily used as a venue for chariot races and equestrian events until the sixth century. From the CPG Archives

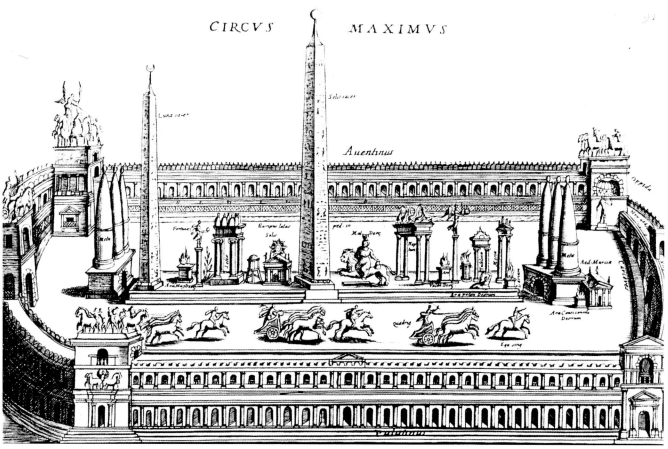

put their logos on every available surface within range of a television camera.

- Thanks to new materials, designs, and technologies, stadiums have adapted to an increased number of uses beyond traditional athletic events such as baseball, football, and track and field. New ground protection materials, for example, make it possible to pack a stadium for a rock concert or a tractor pull on a Friday night and still have the playing surface in shape for a Sunday afternoon football or baseball game. Domes make rain checks as obsolete as the drop kick.
- Finally, there is the matter of cost. Tiger Stadium in Detroit was built in 1912 for $300,000. Today a similar stadium would cost $50 million. Domed stadiums can cost upwards of $500 million, as did Toronto's SkyDome.

Left: The Colosseum at Rome, erected by Vespasian and his son Titus, was dedicated in A.D. 80. Though the upper part of the structure was originally constructed of wood, it was replaced by stone after A.D. 223. At 250 feet long and 151 feet wide, the Roman Colosseum presented gladiatorial contests, wild beast fights, and other spectacles. From the CPG Archives

reality. It is, simultaneously, a giant electronic information center, television screen, entertainment source, and advertising medium.

- Box seats behind home plate or the 50-yard line have given way to climate-controlled luxury suites and premium-priced club seats as the definitive means of taking clients out to the ball game. Luxury suites are also finding their way into college football stadiums and minor-league and spring training baseball parks.
- From edifices built by team owners primarily to attract paying fans from local neighborhoods, stadiums have become symbols of civic pride and accomplishment; a new stadium or "sportsplex" has replaced the skyscraper as testament to a city's, county's, or region's importance. Stadiums have also become "anchors" of urban redevelopment projects, as in Atlanta, Baltimore, and Cleveland.
- Stadiums have grown enormously as an advertising medium. A single stadium can take in up to $5 million a year from consumer product and service marketers who

What is the next phase in the evolution of stadiums, especially as the twenty-first century closes in? What's on the wish list of team owners, stadium authorities, and the others in the business of satisfying the public's ravenous appetite for stadium events?

The short answer is anything that will attract more fans to stadium seats and manage the stadium-going experience. Already in existence: baseball-only stadiums that, like Oriole Park at Camden Yards in Baltimore, Cleveland's Jacobs Field, and Coors Field in Denver, appeal to fan nostalgia for the likes of Ebbets Field (Brooklyn), Sportsman's Park (St. Louis), and Fenway Park (still going strong in Boston). Coming soon, if not

already here: state-of-the-art features such as retractable roofs, convertibility from football to baseball, and amenities, amenities, and more amenities.

For example, already in existence are listening devices for the hearing impaired, individually controlled seat-back TV monitors in club seating areas, meals delivered to premium seats and paid for electronically, and, for holders of outdoor club seats, jet streams of cool air for hot days. This is a far cry from the dirt embankments of ancient Greece or the stadiums and ballparks that prevailed throughout much of the twentieth century.

The stadium got its name as well as its start in ancient Greece. The word *stadion* is derived from the Greek word for a unit of length equal to 606 feet, nine inches, the distance of the original Olympian foot race. The term was later applied to the area where the race was run and then to the terraced rows of seats from which spectators cheered their favorite runners home.

The next stadiums of historical note were the Circus Maximus and Colosseum in Rome. The Colosseum, familiar to moviegoers as the scene of Ben Hur's chariot race and the gladiatorial endeavors of Spartacus, is said to have had an extensive system of underground passages that could be flooded for mock naval battles. If there had been such a thing as baseball in the days of the Emperor Vespasian, the 45,000-seat Colosseum (at 250 feet long and 151 feet wide) would have been a slugger's paradise.

After the fall of Rome, stadiums declined in importance and languished through the Middle Ages to modern times. Even though baseball, football, and other field sports gathered momentum in North America throughout the nineteenth century, they didn't attract enough spectators to warrant the construction of stadiums.

The first modern stadium, seating 66,000, was built in Athens for the revival of the Olympic Games in 1896. The next modern stadium to be built was London's White City Stadium in 1908, also for the Olympic Games. Olympic stadiums followed in Stockholm, Amsterdam, Berlin, and Helsinki. In the United States, the Los Angeles Memorial Coliseum, built in 1923, was enlarged for the 10th Olympiad in 1932.

The trend continues to this day. Atlanta is getting a new stadium for the 1996 Olympics. Built to seat more than 60,000 Olympics spectators, the stadium will be converted into a 45,000-seat baseball-only park

for the Atlanta Braves in 1997.

Serious U.S. stadium construction began in the early twentieth century as baseball and football began to capture the national imagination and the nation's first genuine sports heroes emerged. Where better to capture the essence of this era than the Yale-Harvard rivalry that kicked off intercollegiate football in 1876?

By 1896, wrote Charles A. Ferry, the engineer who designed and supervised the construction of Yale Bowl, "the attendance at Yale games called for special accommodations for spectators at the intercollegiate matches." The solution was to build wooden stands seating 18,000, which soon had to be expanded to accommodate 33,000 spectators. Wrote Ferry in 1916, "These, so far as the writer knows, were the largest wooden stands ever erected."

Enter rival Harvard, upping the ante in 1904 with America's first steel and reinforced concrete stadium and with a seating capacity of 23,000. With its wooden stands ruined by the weather and faced with costly repairs, Yale allocated $235,000 for a steel-and-concrete stadium that could seat 50,000. Thus was born Yale Bowl.

Across the country, in Pasadena, California, the Tournament of Roses Association recognized that the grandstands in a local park were getting too small for the traditional football game following the New Year's Day "Rose Parade" and commissioned a stadium modeled after the Yale Bowl. It is probably no coincidence that the president of the Tournament of Roses Association grew up in New Haven, Connecticut, the site of the Yale Bowl.

Dubbed "The Rose Bowl," the new stadium, which seated 57,000 (it now seats

The Montreal Olympic Stadium, built for the 1976 Summer Olympics, is not only home to the Montreal Expos, but also a multipurpose venue that has hosted a variety of athletic and musical events as well as a Papal visit and numerous trade and consumer exhibitions. Courtesy, Régie des installations olympiques

104,000), was dedicated in 1923 with a game in which the University of Southern California beat Penn State 14-3. Prophetically for Southern Californians, the kickoff was delayed for more than an hour because the Penn State team was stuck in traffic en route to the game.

The Rose Bowl set the style for other college stadiums around the

United States. Schools with seating capacities of more than 50,000 are commonplace, while some Big Ten stadiums' capacities exceed 100,000.

Propelled by the popularity of such great players as Hack Wilson, Ty Cobb, Tris Speaker, Honus Wagner, Cy Young, Walter Johnson, and, of course, Babe Ruth, a first generation of major-league baseball parks appeared on the scene in the years preceding World War I. They became the Colosseums of the New World.

Philadelphia's Shibe Park, America's first fireproof baseball stadium, opened in 1909, as did Forbes Field in Pittsburgh. Akron's League Park, home to the Akron Black Tyrites of the Negro National League, opened in 1910. Griffith

Above: A vintage 1920s advertisement for Yale Bowl shows the stadium's bowl shape that influenced the design of Pasadena's Rose Bowl. Courtesy, Yale University

Right: Touchdown Yale! This photo dating from the 1940s depicts a near-capacity crowd at Yale Bowl. Courtesy, Yale University

Stadium (Washington) and the Polo Grounds (New York) followed in 1911. Cincinnati's Crosley Field, Boston's Fenway Park, and Detroit's Tiger Stadium came on stream in 1912. Ebbets Field, where the singular Brooklyn Dodgers held sway, opened in 1913; Wrigley Field became part of the landscape of Chicago's North Side in 1914; and Braves Field made its debut in Boston in 1915.

These ballparks, constructed of structural steel and concrete that permitted upper decks, were built in the neighborhoods that supported the teams. An article in *Sports History* magazine (defunct since 1989) described the early ballparks in Philadelphia as "Agrarian illusions set like emeralds into a chimney-stacked landscape . . . boxes of grassy respite from the smoke-charred bricks all around."

Into these "boxes of grassy respite" thronged eager fans. Ring Lardner, whose reporting on the early days of modern baseball earned him a permanent place in American letters, described the atmosphere of opening day at Forbes Field in 1909: "The women came dressed as if for the greatest society event of the year . . . Gorgeous gowns, topped by still more gorgeous hats, were in evidence everywhere. Most of the gowns were white and formed a pretty combination with the prevalent green of the stands."

Amenities for fans and players alike were at a premium. Because most stadiums provided changing facilities for the home team only, a visiting team often had to take a streetcar from its hotel to the ballpark in full uniform.

While football stadiums were generally bowl- or oval-shaped, baseball parks came in all shapes and sizes. The size and shape of a

Above: The Rose Bowl, the scene of a post-season intercollegiate football championship held every New Year's Day after the Pasadena Tournament of Roses Parade, was modeled after the Yale Bowl. This postcard depicting the stadium dates from the mid-1930s. From the CPG Archives

Top: This historic postcard depicts Boston's Harvard Stadium, the first steel and reinforced concrete stadium in the United States and home to the Harvard Crimson football team. From the CPG Archives

Charles A. Comiskey, a professional baseball player at the age of 17, became owner and president of the Chicago White Sox in 1900. Nine years later he commissioned architect Zachary Taylor Davis to design a fan-friendly ballpark for his team. Comiskey was posthumously elected to the Baseball Hall of Fame in 1939. From Cirker, *Dictionary of American Portraits,* Dover, 1967

ballpark was, more often than not, determined by its street boundaries. In his foreword to Philip J. Lowry's *Green Cathedrals*, architect Dale Swearingen writes: "The classic ballpark was totally integrated into the neighborhood. A little known but crucial benefit . . . was that ballparks took on an asymmetrical form as dictated by the property lines of the site." In other words, strategies varied with the distance, as decided by property lines, to the left, center, and right field fences of each ballpark.

A stadium's dimensions were not always defined by the configuration of the neighboring streets. Yankees' owner Jacob Ruppert ordered the designers of Yankee Stadium to specify a short right field to accommodate the left-hand hitting Babe Ruth. The "Bambino" justified Ruppert's strategem by hitting his

Cleveland's Municipal Stadium, situated next to Lake Erie, was the site of Opera Week in 1931. Ninety thousand opera lovers attended the concerts, but the stadium's acoustics were more attuned to the crack of the bat than the voice of a tenor. From the CPG Archives

first homer in Yankee Stadium the day it opened, April 18, 1923. The "House that Ruth Built" turned out to be the "House that was Built for Ruth."

Asymmetrical dimensions were not the only eccentricities of this first generation of modern ballparks. The roof of a Philadelphia and Reading Railroad tunnel running under Baker Bowl, one-time home field of the Philadelphia Phillies, made a huge hump in center field.

As soon as modern stadiums began to appear, they became venues for a smorgasbord of events. Yankee Stadium hosted 30 championship fights, 22 Notre Dame-Army football games, 17 years of NFL football with the New York Giants, 18 years of Grambling University football, and decades of rodeos, circuses, pop concerts, religious revivals, and three Papal visits.

Cleveland Stadium in 1931 put on a solid week of opera from *Aida* to *Die Meistersinger,* on what was the largest stage ever constructed for an operatic performance. Although Opera Week, as it was called, drew nearly 90,000 music lovers, disappointing acoustics wrote the finale to the program.

The lights went on in stadiums when the lights went out on the economy—during the Great Depression. The first stadium to be lit up for a night game was Crosley Field in Cincinnati, for a Reds-Phillies game on May 24, 1935. The significance of the occasion was recognized in the highest places, as President Franklin Roosevelt turned on the lights by pushing a button in the White House (500 miles away). The lighting system, which cost $50,000 and shone with more than 600 1,500-watt bulbs, not only lit up the night, but the cash register as well.

The first night game drew 20,000 fans, about 10 times the number the Reds were accustomed to attracting during a lackluster season. It was also a significant step toward what is now called the fan-friendly stadium; night baseball gave fans who couldn't get to day games a chance to root for their heroes under the lights. A less heralded, but equally important fan-friendly innovation of the same era: stadium loudspeakers.

The new generation came on stream with the same rapidity as its predecessor. A dozen new parks opened in as many years. Candlestick Park in San Francisco led the way in 1960, followed by Shea Stadium in Flushing Meadows, Dodger Stadium in Los Angeles' Chavez Ravine, and Robert F. Kennedy Memorial Stadium in Washington, D. C., in

Jacob Ruppert, owner of the New York Yankees, asked the builders of Yankee Stadium for a short right field to accommodate Babe Ruth's left-hand hitting. Ruppert's foresight immediately paid off. When the stadium opened on April 18, 1923, Ruth hit his first home run there. From Cirker, *Dictionary of American Portraits,* Dover, 1967

On January 3, 1962, ground was broken for the Harris County Domed Stadium, now better known as the Houston Astrodome. This architectural marvel, the first of the domed stadiums, opened in 1965. Courtesy, Houston Metropolitan Research Center, Houston Public Library

No longer venues meant only for football or baseball, today's stadiums host an astounding array of events, including rodeos. This shot was taken inside Houston's Astrodome. Photo by Jim McNee / The Stockhouse Inc., Houston

and tremendous exposure to the teams. For their part, the stadiums did their best to accommodate TV with media amenities such as interview rooms for postgame news conferences.

Another influence on the new generation of stadiums was the multiple uses for which stadiums were designed; virtually every stadium built during the sixties and seventies was intended to house both baseball and football teams. Events such as rock concerts, motor sports, and fireworks displays (to name just a few) were sought after to fill stadium's revenue gaps when the baseball and football teams were idle or traveling. This maximum utilization principle led to the new technologies that emerged with the new generation of stadiums, notably artificial turf and domes.

Artificial turf filled the needs of the high-use stadium. It required none of the expensive maintenance of sod; it could be used in all weather; it could endure constant use; and it gave a playing field a sleek, modern look consistent with the new stadiums of the day. Artificial turf also proved to be controversial. Sports purists lamented the departure of natural turf, and some people claimed that

1962, Busch Stadium in St. Louis in 1966, Fulton County Stadium in Atlanta and San Diego Jack Murphy Stadium in 1967, Three Rivers (Pittsburgh) and Riverfront (Cincinnati) stadiums in 1970, Veterans Stadium (Philadelphia) and Foxboro Stadium outside Boston in 1971, and Kansas City's Arrowhead Stadium in 1972.

Several influences were to have a profound effect on the stadiums of this era. The first was television. It brought huge revenues

Astroturf increased the number of knee and leg injuries.

Domed stadiums, climate-controlled and rain-proof, made their debut with the Harris County Domed Stadium, also known as the Houston Astrodome, in 1965. Domes represented the ultimate in fan-friendliness. There were no more rainouts or rain delays and no more frostbitten toes and fingers. Domes were player-friendly as well. Gale-force winds no longer frustrated quarterbacks and punters, and gusts coming in from the outfield no longer turned home run shots into pop flies.

The list of domed stadiums grew quickly through the seventies and eighties and includes the Kingdome (Seattle), Louisiana Superdome (New Orleans), RCA Dome, formerly the Hoosier Dome (Indianapolis),

SkyDome (Toronto), ThunderDome of St. Petersburg, Pontiac Silverdome, Georgia Dome (Atlanta), and the Hubert H. Humphrey Metrodome (Minneapolis-St. Paul).

Today's domes are nothing if not versatile. A sample listing of events at Seattle's Kingdome gives some idea of how versatile. In addition to being home to the Seahawks (football) and Mariners (baseball), the Kingdome has played host to the following: professional and international soccer matches, rodeos, NBA basketball, horse shows, antique shows, religious crusades, political rallies, college basketball and baseball, international volleyball tournaments, big-name rock concerts, circuses, motor sports, and paper airplane contests among many others.

The third and most recent generation in

Minneapolis' Hubert H. Humphrey Metrodome is America's largest air-supported, multiple-use stadium. Ground was broken for the facility in December of 1979, and it was officially opened on April 3, 1982. Photo by James Blank / Scenics of America

Cleveland's Jacobs Field, the Indians' new home, fits neatly into the cityscape. Courtesy, HOK Sports Facilities Group

the evolution of stadiums is an attempt to resurrect the feel of the urban parks of yesteryear (but with all the modern conveniences of today). Facilities such as Oriole Park at Camden Yards in Baltimore, Jacobs Field in Cleveland, and Coors Field in Denver are smaller (about 45,000 capacity) and made for baseball only. They have natural playing surfaces and many of the design features are reminiscent of the early generation of urban ballparks. (The seats at Camden Yards appear to be made of green wood, but closer inspection reveals them to be plastic.)

At the same time, the postmodern ballparks offer luxury suites and club seating,

food courts, and kiddie corners. Coming on stream soon are stadiums with retractable domes in Atlanta, Phoenix, and Seattle (to name three) that will allow fans to enjoy the weather or be protected from it. As stadiums of the sixties and seventies generation undergo renovation, there is a perceptible move back to natural playing surfaces.

The next evolutionary step for stadiums will be determined by market forces. The single most potent market force is the public's growing demand for high-quality, fan-friendly facilities that will justify moving from off the couch in front of the TV screen and into the stadium seat.

▶ Stadium Managers Association

OUR NAME IS THE NAME OF THE GAME!

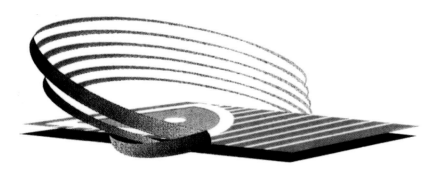

Our objectives are . . .

- *to advance, foster, and promote the professional and effective management of stadiums and similar facilities;*

- *to consider and deal with common intra-industry problems of management;*

- *to investigate and encourage activities aimed at enabling the industry to conduct itself with the greatest efficiency and economy;*

- *to promote free intercourse and dialogue among its members and to give proper consideration and expression of opinion upon questions affecting the industry;*

- *to acquire, assemble, preserve, and disseminate valuable business information;*

- *to adopt standards of conduct and operation for the industry; and*

- *to promote the general welfare of the industry . . .*

For more information, contact:
Stadium Managers Association
875 Kings Highway
Woodbury, NJ 08096-3172
609/845-7220
609/853-0411 (fax)

▶ Coopers & Lybrand L.L.P.

"Not just knowledge. Know-how." More than a phrase or a tag line, these words underscore how Coopers & Lybrand's professionals work to exceed client expectations. ⚑ *At Coopers & Lybrand, knowledge is derived from many sources and know-how takes on many forms throughout its*

consulting practice. Knowledge of the sports and entertainment industry is the basis of the firm's ability to develop effective project analysis and development strategies. Know-how is derived from vast experience serving clients in large and small markets throughout the country and around the world.

In the midst of the constantly shifting sports industry landscape, one aspect remains unchanged: Coopers & Lybrand's commitment to quality, initia-

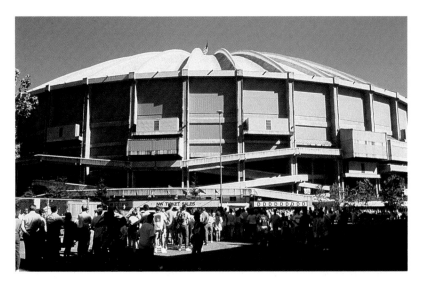

tive, and teamwork. It is a commitment that truly reflects the fundamental values that have been part of the firm since it was formed nearly 100 years ago and is the cornerstone of its success. Concern for clients' welfare, outstanding professional skills, and mutual respect for colleagues—these principles have facilitated its growth, enabling the practice to flourish.

Coopers & Lybrand's Sports, Entertainment & Leisure Consulting Group has been providing consulting services since the late 1970s. *In serving its clients, the group draws from its in-depth understanding of the real world—from how big business is shaping professional sports to how professional sports are*

shaping our society. To date, Coopers & Lybrand is proud to have provided a wide variety of services to more than 170 professional sports and other public assembly facility projects throughout the United States, Canada, South America, Mexico, and the United Kingdom.

The firm's history in this industry dates back to the origins of luxury seat-based financing mechanisms for professional sports facilities. Coopers & Lybrand was involved in the early stages of this trend, providing key financial analysis for the late Joe Robbie that resulted in the development of Joe Robbie Stadium in Miami, Florida.

As the demands on the professional sports industry changed, so did the character of the sports facility. Throughout the late 1970s and into the mid-1980s, the multipurpose stadium, domed and open-air, was in vogue. While not as aesthetic as today's recently developed venues, the stadiums constructed during this period played an important role in the evolution of the sports facility. Premium seating concepts were refined, and the importance of the sports franchise within a community was firmly established. Throughout this period, Coopers & Lybrand remained very active, providing market and financial consulting services from projects including the Hubert H. Humphrey Metrodome in Minneapolis and the RCA Dome in Indianapolis.

More recently, the environment of professional sports facility development has changed dramatically. Single-purpose stadiums and state-of-the-art arenas are the norm. The recent wave of sports facility development has carried with it some interesting statistics:

• Since 1989 seven MLB stadiums have been built or are currently under construction.
• Nearly 60 percent of all existing MLB franchises have recently addressed or are reviewing their current facility needs.
• Since 1987 six NFL stadiums have been built, or are

action, Coopers & Lybrand consultants maintain regular contact with government agencies, professional associations, and other organizations to keep abreast of legislation, changes in regulations, and advances in technology that affect the professional sports industry. Further, its industry group personnel support each practice office with specialized education and attention. By doing their homework, Coopers & Lybrand professionals have a better understanding of today's issues and can more confidently anticipate tomorrow's challenges.

The firm's informed specialists and available resources benefit its clients at times such as these—when the complexities of professional sports and facility development, financing, and ownership are expanding at an accelerating rate. It is during these times that the decision-making process demands the judgment of experienced specialists embodied with the highest professional standards. The skills possessed within Coopers & Lybrand's Sports, Entertainment & Leisure Consulting Group result from years of experience in assessing financial, market, economic, and utilization matters. This diverse background has been instrumental in enabling the firm to provide its clients with a thorough understanding of the numerous facets and challenges of the professional sports industry.

Coopers & Lybrand's Sports, Entertainment & Leisure Consulting Group has provided consulting services for stadium renovation and development projects such as Detroit's Tiger Stadium (above), Cleveland's Jacobs Field (left), and Seattle's Kingdome (facing page), among many others.

currently under construction or undergoing substantial renovation.
• Over 60 percent of all existing NFL franchises have recently addressed or are reviewing their current facility needs.

Throughout this new era in facility development, Coopers & Lybrand has been a leader in providing consulting services. Professional sports facilities, including the new MLB ballpark in Cleveland, the NFL stadium in St. Louis, potential stadium developments in Milwaukee and Detroit, and Minor League ballparks throughout the country, have benefited from the firm's market, financial, economic, and operational consulting services.

Supported by Coopers & Lybrand's firmly established roots in financial services, the sports group has gained extensive experience preparing detailed revenue and expense projections, assessing and recommending optimal financing alternatives, analyzing and reviewing various financing strategies, analyzing the costs/benefits of financing options, and assisting in the development of public/private financial packages. In addition, it has been involved in numerous studies focusing on market supply and demand analysis, facility site analysis, economic impact, development planning, and valuation services. The firm has been fortunate in being able to assist many prestigious clients throughout the era of mixed-use, multipurpose stadiums and into the latest generation of modern stadium development.

To remain in the vanguard of thought and

SPORTS, ENTERTAINMENT, AND LEISURE SERVICES
During Planning, Construction, and Operations...

- ► Market Analysis
- ► Facility Design Criteria
- ► Financial Operating Analysis
- ► Economic Impact
- ► Funding Plan Analysis
- ► Site Analysis
- ► Litigation Support
- ► Marketing Strategies

- ► Management/Operations Review
- ► Cash Flow Improvement
- ► Engineering/Construction Support
- ► Master Planning
- ► Valuation Services
- ► Ancillary Facilities Analysis
- ► Contract Negotiation
- ► Facility Management Selection

Coopers &Lybrand

▶ Huber, Hunt & Nichols, Inc.

Huber, Hunt & Nichols has constructed more stadiums and mass seating facilities than any other firm in the United States. This 50-year-old construction manager and general building contractor has, for the past 30 years, been actively involved in building many of the stadiums

Construction manager and general contractor Huber, Hunt & Nichols built Jacobs Field (right) and Joe Robbie Stadium (below), among many others.

and arenas in use today.

Huber, Hunt & Nichols is headquartered in Indianapolis, Indiana, and maintains large regional offices in Branchburg, New Jersey; Dallas, Texas; and Phoenix, Arizona. The company is privately held.

Indiana University's football stadium was the first major facility built by the firm. This project was followed by four stadiums all built by Huber, Hunt & Nichols as a general contractor. These include the 57,000-seat Riverfront Stadium, the 57,000-seat Three Rivers Stadium, the 85,000-seat Superdome, and the 50,000-seat University of Kentucky Stadium. These projects were followed by the firm's first design/build stadium—the 41,000-seat facility for Iowa State University.

In the mid-1970s Huber, Hunt & Nichols built, as a construction manager, the 50,000-seat Carrier Dome in Syracuse, New York. This project was one of the early prototypes for air-supported domes. The 50,000-seat West Virginia Stadium followed the Carrier Dome and at this time Huber, Hunt & Nichols was becoming known as the premier builder of stadiums throughout the United States. Huber, Hunt & Nichols was then asked to assist the Province of British Columbia in the construction of its new 50,000-seat British Columbia Place. The firm worked closely with the contractor, Dillingham, as well as with the owner

to bring the project in on time and within budget.

This project was followed by the 76,000-seat Joe Robbie Stadium in Miami, Florida. Huber, Hunt & Nichols was then requested to be construction manager for the renovation and expansion of the Liberty Bowl in Memphis, Tennessee. The 43,000-seat ThunderDome in St. Petersburg, Florida, and the 45,000-seat AlamoDome in San Antonio, Texas, were the next two major stadium projects built by Huber, Hunt & Nichols. The firm was then hired by the Gateway Corporation as construction managers to build the 43,000-seat Jacobs Field project in Cleveland, Ohio.

At the time of this printing the firm is currently building the 83,000-seat stadium for the Jacksonville Jaguars in Jacksonville, Florida, and the new home for the Phoenix Major League Baseball expansion team.

In addition to the above-referenced stadiums, Huber, Hunt & Nichols, Inc., has constructed 17 major arenas in North America, all of which are in use today.

All of the above-mentioned facilities have been built on time and within the owners' budget. Huber, Hunt & Nichols is extremely proud of these accomplishments throughout the years and looks forward to exciting opportunities in the future.

▶ Stein & Company

Stein & Company is a comprehensive real estate services firm noted for development expertise on a wide range of sports and assembly facilities nationally. Stein & Company specializes in distinctive, large-scale projects with an emphasis on public-sector real estate.

The organization, with more than 240 personnel and a Program Management staff of more than 50 members, provides a deep resource base that brings innovative, client-driven solutions to each engagement.

The focus of Stein & Company's Program Management sports, convention center, and entertainment practice is to provide real estate consulting and development services to facility owners and users, municipalities, investors, and financial institutions for successful management of high-profile, complex projects. The group's program managers serve as an extension of the client's staff, bringing the following benefits:

- *Superior knowledge* of building types and development process
- An *established methodology for controlling development risk* in dollars and schedule
- Predevelopment expertise, including *market and financial feasibility analyses*
- *Budget development and financial modeling* required to defensibly predict success
- *A strong network* of consultants, contractors, and lending institutions
- Expertise in *architectural and construction contract negotiations* and administration
- A history of *on-time, on-budget project management performance*

Facilities in which Stein & Company has been engaged include:

- Jacksonville Stadium
- Comiskey Park
- McCormick Place Convention Center
- CoreStates Center
- Tucson Convention Center
- United Center
- Monona Terrace Convention Center
- The Rose Garden
- Upstate Arena
- Winnipeg SuperPlex
- Calgary Convention Center
- Milwaukee Exposition Convention Center & Arena
- Loyola University of Chicago, Lake Shore

Clients engage Stein & Company because they know that, as developers and managers of more than $4.5 billion in real estate undertakings, the firm fully understands the business, especially the development and financial risks associated with projects of large scale. Stein & Company empowers the client team with knowledge of the specific product and process, offering greater certainty in a major investment. The result is mitigated risk and maximized contributions made by all parties throughout the development cycle. Ultimately, the client achieves substantial savings through Stein & Company's program management assistance.

For further information regarding these specialized services, contact Vincent P. Ziolkowski, senior vice president/program management, or Charles H. Johnson, vice president/program management, at 312/372-4240. Or write to them at:

Stein & Company
227 West Monroe St., Ste. 3400
Chicago, IL 60606

Jacksonville Stadium (above) and United Center (below left) are just two of the facilities in which Stein & Company has been engaged.

*S*tately, neoclassic Soldier Field rises above Chicago's colorful Burnham Park Marina. Photo by James Blank / Scenics of America

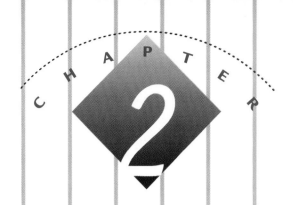
STADIUM ARCHITECTURE

Designs to Get Fans Into the Seats

Any discussion of stadium architecture today must begin with a retelling of the ancient tale of the blind men and the elephant, in which four sightless men stand around an elephant, debating its shape and size. One touches its trunk and says an elephant resembles a snake. Another touches its tail and says an elephant clearly is shaped like a rope. The man who touches the elephant's leg likens the pachyderm to a tree. And the fourth fellow walks into the elephant's side and says he's hit a wall.

Architects and engineers designing today's stadiums and ballparks face a similar challenge. A stadium comprises seats, suites, aisles, lights, playing surfaces, portals, press boxes, ramps, rest rooms, steel girders, and reinforced concrete, all packaged to meet the expectations and priorities of a potpourri of stadium constituencies.

Team owners, stadium and sports authorities, and politicians want revenues, recognition, civic pride, and, increasingly, focal points for downtown revitalization programs. Government agencies such as sports and stadium authorities look for facilities that can accommodate as many revenue-producing uses as possible in addition to serving as the home field of a big-league football and baseball team. Privately owned stadiums tend to favor one sport—the one played by the stadium owner's team—relegating other tenants to a secondary role in their plans.

Business executives want luxury accommodations in which to entertain and be entertained. Some stadium luxury suites are popular lunch and dining spots even when there's no game.

Coaches and players want well-maintained playing fields, first-rate locker rooms, saunas, weight and training rooms, x-ray rooms, whirlpools, and, with growing frequency, lap pools as well as batting rooms equipped with pitching machines.

The media want comfortable press boxes with the latest components of the information superhighway, interview rooms, TV-camera platforms, adequate TV cable hookups, and even darkroom facilities for still photographers. TV sports producers have their say in stadium design, advising on such mediacentric considerations as camera angles, placement of advertising signs, and the number of bays to accommodate broadcast trucks. The internationalization of many North American sports events such as the Super Bowl, World Series, and World Cup soccer, require additional media facilities for foreign TV crews.

This luxury suite at Joe Robbie Stadium sports all the amenities of home and more! Courtesy, HOK Sports Facilities Group

Locker rooms have taken on a clean, modern look as evidenced by this view of the Dolphins' changing facility at Joe Robbie Stadium. Courtesy, HOK Sports Facilities Group

Some college stadiums rival their professional counterparts in the amenities department as evidenced by this view of recently completed executive suites and a press box at the University of Tennessee's Neyland Stadium. Courtesy, University of Tennessee, Knoxville

What do fans want? In a word, everything, if they are going to be coaxed off their living room couches and into stadium seats.

Reflecting nineties sensibilities, fans want a family-friendly environment with amenities such as more numerous and accessible lavatories (including more women's facilities and diaper-changing tables in both men's and women's rooms) and more concession stands with menus that are as likely to offer sushi and salad as hot dogs and hamburgers. The ratio of concession stands to customers already has dropped precipitously from one per 1,000 a decade ago to one for every 200 today. Architects say future stadiums will have a concession stand for every 150 patrons.

Increasingly, fans want attractions for kids. Thirty-plus-year-old Shea Stadium in New York joined with Nickelodeon, a cable network known for children's shows and sitcom reruns, to open a 25,000-square-foot interactive theme park behind the stadium's right field wall. The Ballpark at Arlington,

Texas, which became the Texas Rangers' new home in 1994, caters to young people with a youth park and a learning center.

Fans want to be close to the action on the playing field, not only during the game, but also during pregame rituals such as calisthenics, pitchers' warm-ups, and batting practice. In an extravagant display of team spirit and/or baseball mania, 40,000 Texas Rangers fans paid to see their team work out at The Ballpark at Arlington.

Fans also want the stadium to be as much an experience as the game itself. They crave feelings of intimacy and nostalgia, best supplied in baseball venues such as Baltimore's critically and commercially successful Oriole Park at Camden Yards, Chicago's Comiskey Park, Cleveland's Jacobs Field, and, in the minors, Buffalo's Pilot Field, the design of which integrates snugly with the historic district surrounding it.

Vocally reviling and rejecting what have come to be known as the "ashtray" generation stadiums of the sixties, fans demand real

grass rather than artificial turf and masonry that evokes the brick-and-stone and gingerbread detail of bygone days instead of the stark concrete structures set in the middle of parking lots. They not only want excellent views of the playing field, but also picture postcard vistas of the surrounding neighborhood, such as the historic Bromo-Seltzer clock down the block from Baltimore's Oriole Park at Camden Yards and Denver's historic quarter below Coors Field, where the Colorado Rockies begin play in 1995.

All architectural decisions are driven by the overriding issues of sports economics and marketing. With a cost of $120 million to $200 million just to open its doors, a stadium has to start generating revenues even before the first shovel breaks ground. The cash cow of choice is premium seating for season ticket holders from climate-controlled, poshly furnished luxury boxes to less elaborate club seats—leases at prices ranging from the low five figures to $200,000 per season. As an example of just how much premium seating can help a franchise, the Carolina Panthers, a new National Football League franchise in the Charlotte, North Carolina, region, astounded a dubious NFL brass and got a flying start on its 72,000-seat stadium by garnering income of $30 million from the advance sale of suite and club seating for its maiden season.

The stadium must also be designed with the flexibility to accommodate a great enough variety of ancillary events (e.g., conventions, concerts, circuses, motor sports, rodeos, religious revivals) to maintain a

steady year-long revenue stream. Domed stadiums built adjacent to convention and civic centers have the advantage of versatility. They can be quickly converted into convention exhibition sites and, with the addition of seats, can be adapted for basketball. Indianapolis' RCA Dome and Atlanta's Georgia Dome are two current examples. A domed stadium-convention center opened in St. Louis in time for the 1995 football season.

Also on the minds of those charged with defining the stadiums of the nineties and the coming century:

• Giving stadiums memorable signature identities that sell seats and attract TV coverage by making the ballpark a bigger star than the ballplayers and a destination in itself
• Keeping costs down by specifying low-maintenance materials such as durable, easy-to-clean precast concrete exteriors designed to simulate more expensive masonry, slatted plastic seats constructed and painted to look like wood, and, in the case of covered stadiums, fiberglass and Teflon-coated, fiberglass-reinforced fabric translucent domes that give fans a feeling of being outdoors. (The translucent dome at

Poshly furnished luxury suites such as this one at Camden Yards generate a substantial amount of revenue for stadiums. Courtesy, HOK Sports Facilities Group

The Americans with Disabilities Act mandates that one percent of the seating capacity of a stadium must be allocated for wheelchair spaces. Courtesy, HOK Sports Facilities Group

Facing page: Critically acclaimed and commercially successful Oriole Park at Camden Yards stands within close proximity to Baltimore's landmark Bromo-Seltzer clock. Courtesy, HOK Sports Facilities Group

the Pontiac Silverdome let in enough sun to temporarily nourish natural sod for its round of 1994 World Cup soccer matches.) Cost considerations limit some otherwise appealing architectural features. Retractable roofs, the most prominent example of which is Toronto's SkyDome, can keep out the sun, rain, or cold, but can also cost $50 million to $100 million to build.

• Designing flexibility into a stadium by building in convertibility from one sport or event to another. Case in point: Atlanta's

Olympic Stadium, built to hold 85,000 spectators for the 1996 Olympics, will be reconfigured to a 45,000-seat ballpark for the Atlanta Braves baseball team in 1997. Some minor-league ballparks, such as Pilot Field (Buffalo), Charlotte Knights Baseball Stadium, and a forthcoming park for the AAA Rochester (New York) Redwings, are designed to be upgraded to major-league parks if a major-league franchise comes to town.

• Complying with a lengthening list of local,

Pilot Field, Buffalo's minor-league ballpark, was designed by HOK Sports Facilities Group to be upgraded to a major-league park. Courtesy, HOK Sports Facilities Group

state, and federal regulations covering everything from fire safety to accommodation of the disabled. The Americans with Disabilities Act (ADA), for example, mandates that wheelchair spaces constitute one percent of a stadium's seating capacity; a 70,000-seat stadium, for example, must have 700 wheelchair spaces integrated into the general seating areas. Architects estimate that this requirement increases a stadium's size by 5 to 10 percent. As for fire regulations, Chicago's new Comiskey Park,

opened in 1991, had to incorporate a sprinkler system because city fire codes classified it as a high-rise building.

Randy Dvorak, a senior vice president of Hellmuth, Obata & Kassenbaum (HOK), a Kansas City, Missouri, architectural firm well-known for its work in sports facilities, sums up the state of stadium architecture and design today when he says: "It's amazing what you have to create over and above the spectator accommodations."

Some things about spectacular accommodations remain the same no matter what else changes about stadiums. As it was in ancient Greece, the crucial determinant of a stadium's success is its sight lines, the view of the playing field from all the seats.

The angle of most stadium seating ranges from 30-38 degrees, a comfortable pitch made possible by the fact that spectators are looking between and not over the heads of the people in front of them. Forcing spectators to look *over* the heads of the people in front of them would make seating angles uncomfortably steep.

A common device used by stadium designers to reduce sight line distance while minimizing the pitch of the seats is to put the floor of the stadium as much as 30 feet below street level. The result is that spectators enter the stadium from the street at about

The Yale Bowl (marked here for the Yale-Harvard game) was designed by architect Charles A. Ferry, who believed that oval-shaped stadiums enabled "each spectator to obtain a view of the entire audience, a very thrilling spectacle when . . . everyone is roused to a high pitch of excitement by some brilliant play." Courtesy, Yale University

mezzanine level and are spared a steep climb to upper deck seats.

More and more, stadium architects are sitting down to the personal computer to arrive at optimum sight lines for a stadium. In designing the new Comiskey Park for the Chicago White Sox, designers at HOK used PC software written in-house to analyze sight lines and sections for the upper deck, balancing the desire to keep seats close to the field with the need to keep seating tiers from rising too steeply.

An important, but little-mentioned, aspect of stadium design is the spectators' views of each other. Listen again to Yale Bowl architect Charles A. Ferry in his prescient paper delivered to the American Society of Civil Engineers in 1916: "The [oval] form [of the bowl] enables each spectator to obtain a view of the entire audience, a very thrilling spectacle when all the seats are filled and everyone is roused to a high pitch of excitement by some brilliant play."

Sight lines are different for football and baseball, raising a question of compatibility of the two sports. The baseball field is basically square (even allowing for the asymmetrical designs of many ballparks), its sight line focusing on the infield diamond. Football is a rectangular game, where the action moves between end zones. Both sports shared facilities when there were fewer teams, shorter seasons, and less likelihood of schedule conflicts. Pro football, until its expansion in the sixties, was the junior partner and had to make do running off-tackle plays on pitcher's mounds and base paths.

When pro football caught fire in the sixties, teams were attracting crowds in excess of 60,000, far too many for most baseball parks. The result was a new generation of football-only stadiums, starting with Arrowhead Stadium in Kansas City, which opened in 1972. Baseball's response was the distinctive retro-genre parks that have been generating so much excitement.

Terry Miller, director of sports architecture with Howard Needles Tammen and Bergendoff (HNTB) of Kansas City, sums it up by saying, "The movement these days is against making those football-baseball places that serve both games. It's best to build a park for one or the other, because if you don't, one sport will always suffer."

Even though the new baseball parks have been received enthusiastically, there is some disagreement among designers about stadium structure. One frequently aired issue is columns versus no columns.

A bit of history: many of the early stadiums (Yankee Stadium, Fenway Park, and Polo Grounds among them) were designed and built by Frank Osborn, a Cleveland engineer primarily known as a bridge builder. Employing what would be called technology transfer today, Osborn used steel girders customarily used as bridge trusses to support upper decks of stadiums. The result was the classic ballpark look that is enjoying a renaissance today. While columns brought occupants of the upper deck closer to the action on the field, they had one notorious drawback: Whoever sat behind them didn't see much of the game.

Precast concrete did away with the need for columns, but also forced architects to design upper decks farther back from the field. It wasn't feasible to build a steeply vertical stadium without columns. So while there were no obstructed views, spectators in upper-deck seats were more likely to need binoculars.

The pro-column side says the steeper structure made possible by steel columns brings thousands of people closer to the action on the field, while blocking the view of only a few hundred. And besides, column advocates say, how often is a stadium so crowded that people are forced to have their views ruined by columns?

The anti-column side rests its case on the notion that columns are a step backward—and an expensive one at that.

Stadiums are a form of civic architecture,

putting them in the same category as courthouses or state capitols. But there the similarity ends. A stadium on a game day projects festiveness, excitement, and anticipation that are heightened by its forms, textures, and colors. Coaches and managers swear that a new stadium raises a team's level of play. Fans feel unbounded confidence, justified or not, in their team.

Rick deFlon, former vice president of Ellerbe Becket, another Kansas City architectural firm with a strong reputation in sta-

Though the players have not yet taken the field, excitement and anticipation are in the air at the ballpark in the minutes before game time. Courtesy, HOK Sports Facilities Group

dium design, says there is no book on how to design a stadium, and that every assignment presents an entirely unique set of challenges.

In an appraisal of The Ballpark at Arlington, Paul Goldberger, an architectural writer who is now chief cultural correspondent for *The New York Times*, gives his impression of the impact a stadium has on a fan. After describing the park's exterior and surroundings, he writes: "The magic moment . . . is when you step through the stone arches and catch a glimpse of the field within: It is a powerful instant when you feel the order of the city and the order of baseball coming together."

Background: This plan of Coors Field shows the dimensions of the stadium's natural turf playing field. Courtesy, HOK Sports Facilities Group

▶ HOK Sports Facilities Group

Hellmuth, Obata and Kassabaum's Sports Facilities Group (HOK Sport)

keeps setting new records in sports facilities design. The Kansas City-based

architectural firm has developed an international reputation for its

design work, which includes more than 250 sports-related facilities.

On its roster: Miami's Joe Robbie Stadium. Baltimore's Oriole Park at Camden Yards. Chicago's United Center, home to the NBA Bulls and NHL Blackhawks. And most recently, Denver's Coors Field, home to the Colorado Rockies. In fact, you would be hard-pressed to name a sports facility where HOK

Sport or its personnel have not played a major role.

HOK Sport's success in this unique niche is based upon a simple formula: Love of sport plus love of architecture equals great sports architecture. Ron Labinski, FAIA, senior vice president and himself an avowed sports enthusiast, realized long ago that sports fans made the best sports facilities designers. In 1983 Labinski and several colleagues, all of whom had worked together on sports-related projects since the early 1970s, decided to start a firm devoted exclusively to sports architecture. When the St. Louis-based Hellmuth, Obata and Kassabaum, Inc., learned of the group's plans, it offered association. That association has proven beneficial to both: HOK is now the

largest architectural firm in the United States, and HOK Sport is by far the largest and best-known firm in the world specializing in sports architecture.

Over the years, HOK Sport has developed an impressive client list. Under the heading of "National Football League" are the names of 28 of 30 franchises. Under "Major League Baseball," 22 of 28 teams. Numerous Minor League teams. More than 45 colleges and universities. NBA and NHL teams. Sponsors of world-class sporting events. The list goes on and on.

HOK Sport's experience working with the NFL is especially impressive. Beginning with the groundbreaking Joe Robbie Stadium, which opened to rave reviews in 1987, the firm's experience has grown to include new stadia and training facilities, as well as renovations and expansions of existing facilities. Given the depth of its experience, it is no surprise that all five cities vying for a new NFL franchise in 1993 had asked HOK Sport to design their new facility, should they secure a franchise. The winners? Jacksonville and Charlotte. The result? Two new world-class, HOK Sport-designed facilities—Jaguar Stadium in Jacksonville, due to open for the 1995 season, and the Carolinas NFL Stadium, set to open the following season. Another new stadium, the St. Louis Domed Stadium, will open in 1995 as well, and will be the new home for the NFL's Rams.

The firm's track record with Major League Baseball is equally enviable. The best new ballparks in the country: Oriole Park at Camden Yards, for the Baltimore Orioles. Jacobs Field, for the Cleveland Indians. Comiskey Park, for the Chicago White Sox. Coors Field, for the Colorado Rockies. Each designed specifically for its unique setting; each sharing a profound love and respect for the national pastime. According to Joseph E. Spear, AIA, senior vice president, each site evoked a different response. "Baltimore and Cleveland, for example, are both urban ballparks, but they're dramatically different buildings," Spear says. "That difference arises from the special character of each city. What's appropriate in Balti-more wouldn't work in Cleveland."

In addition, the firm has designed a number of Minor League ballparks, including the new Durham Bulls Athletic Park, for the Durham Bulls, Franklin Quest Field, for the Salt Lake City Buzz, and Harbor Park, for the Norfolk Tides. HOK Sport has also made its mark designing spring training facilities for both the Cactus and Grapefruit leagues. In 1994, for example, the firm celebrated the opening of the Peoria Spring Training Facility. It was another first for HOK Sport: The first facility designed specifi-cally to accommodate two Major League teams, the Seattle Mariners and San Diego Padres. According to Earl E. Santee, AIA, senior vice president, the decision made sense for all involved. The teams were able to share in the expens-es, and the city and county benefit by having a game played every day of the spring season. "We had sever-al groups to satisfy, including the owners and tenants, and I think everyone was pleased with the result," Santee says.

While the firm has developed an impressive ros-ter of NFL and Major and Minor League Baseball clients, the list does not end there. HOK Sport has also achieved success designing sports facilities around the world. Most recently, the firm designed the new Hong Kong Stadium, a 40,000-seat facility that hosts Hong Kong's most popular sporting event—the internationally renowned Invitation Rugby Sevens Tournament. Across the Atlantic, the firm has also executed a trio of well-received facilities in England—the National Indoor Arena for Sport in Birmingham, the Sheffield Arena, and the National Cycling Center in Manchester.

"Sport is truly an international language," Labinski explains. "The needs of the fans are always a constant. Identifying the specific needs of the sport is the key to success. And I think we've proven our knowledge and ability, whatever the sport."

Back at home, HOK Sport has designed arenas for clients in the NHL and NBA, among others. The firm designed Milwaukee's Bradley Center, home to the

NBA Bucks and IHL Admirals, which opened in 1988. This landmark facility provided many features that have now become industry standards, including a variety of seating configurations, achieved with retractable and movable seating, as well as a separate luxury suite level. The firm's arena portfolio has grown to include Anaheim's Arrowhead Duck Pond and Chicago's United Center. On the horizon? The stunning new Nashville Arena, as much a performing arts center as a sports venue, that will open in 1996, and Denver's new Pepsi Center, set to open in 1997.

Most would agree that HOK Sport's achievements in professional sports facili-ties design are unmatched. Equally unri-valed is its record with colleges and universities, where the firm has provided everything from master planning ser-vices to new facilities design for more than 45 schools nationwide. "Collegiate projects may be smaller in scale," explains Richard A. Martin, AIA, vice president, "but they are often just as complex." Satisfying the needs of both recreational and athletic department users often presents unique challenges, as do budgetary requirements and construction scheduling issues.

One outstanding example is the Bob Carpenter Sports/Convocation Center at the University of Delaware. The building accommo-dates athletic depart-ment

HOK Sport has received international acclaim for its diverse and innovative architecture, including such projects as the Hong Kong Stadium (facing page), which received a 1995 Honor Award from the American Institute of Architects; the Nashville Arena (below); and Denver's Coors Field (left).

competition, practice and training, recreational sports usage, the university's commencement exercises, and commercial events such as concerts and trade shows. HOK Sport's collegiate portfolio also includes the Reily Student Recreation Center at Tulane University in New Orleans, Byrd Stadium renovations for the University of Maryland at College Park, and the Ben Hill Griffin Stadium Expansion at the University of Florida. The latest? The new Recreational/Sports Facility and Natatorium at Miami University in Ohio, which boasts one of the finest intercollegiate swimming facilities in North America.

Whether professional or collegiate, facilities today are being designed to provide fan-friendly options to suit every taste and budget. HOK Sport first debuted its unique Club Lounge concept at Miami's Joe Robbie Stadium. Since then, the firm has continued to lead the way with innovative amenities designed to please fans and generate much-needed revenue. Party suites. Dugout suites. Club seating with in-seat service. Pre-game picnic and party areas. Restaurants, bars, shops, and entertainment areas— all located inside the stadium. More concession stands, with a wider selection of food and drink. Concession stands and play areas designed especially for children. Souvenir shops. Video arcades. Hall of Fame museums.

Along the way HOK Sport has created another niche—interior design. Whether it's an upscale environment to pamper corporate sponsors, or friendly, colorful interiors and graphics to enliven public spaces, HOK Sport always provides a solution designed to please. The firm's interiors department collaborates with each project team to create interior spaces that reinforce the overall building design. According to Susan Carter, associate and interiors director, enhancing the sports experience is one of the group's major objectives. "There's always a way to bring the excitement and energy of the sports experience into an interior, whether you're working with marble and leather or ceramic tile and paint," Carter says. "That's what makes our work so chal-

lenging—and so much fun."

Planning is another essential component of the firm's comprehensive design approach. According to Craig Meyer, ASLA, vice president, resolution of site-related issues is a key ingredient in a successful project. "Integration into the existing context, whether it's an open landscape or an urban neighborhood, requires a lot of careful thought and hard work early in the project," says Meyer. HOK Sport's planning staff tackles projects ranging from site planning for small projects, such as Minor League ballparks, to master planning for urban districts, college campuses, and Olympic games.

Architecture. Interiors. Planning. Over the past decade HOK Sport has grown from an original staff of eight to more than 160 professionals in a number of design-related disciplines. "Our only focus

A tale of two cities: Brick arches in Baltimore (right); articulated steel connections in Cleveland (far right). Both projects received an Honor Award from the American Institute of Architects.

A super trio of bowls: HOK Sport is the architect of the three newest NFL stadiums: The St. Louis Domed Stadium and Jacksonville's Jaguar Stadium, both of which open in 1995; and the Carolinas NFL Stadium in Charlotte, scheduled to open in 1996 (inset, left to right). The firm's Joe Robbie Stadium (seen beyond) opened in 1987.

is sports facilities architecture, and the fact that we are at the forefront in this field is not an accident," says Dennis R. Wellner, AIA, senior vice president. "We have the best people, and they make it happen."

HOK Sport organizes its staff much like a well-run sports franchise, with both special teams and utility players. "We recognize the need for specialization," says James F. Walters, AIA, senior vice president. "The needs of a Minor League ballpark, for example, and an NBA arena are completely different, so naturally we approach their design differently." A typical design team would include a project designer and project manager with extensive experience in the given building type, working with a project team assembled for its specific technical expertise. This approach works because of the diversity and depth of the firm's staff, and allows them to take on any kind of sports project, anywhere in the world.

The recognition for HOK Sport's work extends well beyond the world of sports. The firm's design work has received an honor extended only to the

privileged few: the Honor Award for Architecture from the American Institute, the profession's highest award. HOK Sport has received this award not once, but three times in two years. The first award, for Oriole Park at Camden Yards, came in 1994. Subsequently, Hong Kong Stadium and Jacobs Field were accorded the same honor in 1995. Not just a rare feat in sports architecture, but a rare feat in architecture. And a lasting reminder that, as in Labinski's original vision, great sports architecture arises from a love of sport combined with a love of architecture.

The future continues to be bright for the dedicated, enthusiastic, and committed sports fans at HOK Sport. The firm's attention to detail and sensitivity to context makes each of its projects "better than the last, more attuned to its surroundings and spectators," notes Deborah Dietsch, editor-in-chief of *Architecture* magazine. Labinski concurs. "Our next project is always our best one," he says. "We're always looking to improve on what we've already done."

▶ Daktronics, Inc.

Every sports facility is unique. Providing a scoring and display system that fits a facility requires careful consideration, adequate technical resources, a wide range of products, and support after the sale. 🏴 *Daktronics, Inc., of Brookings, South Dakota, puts its engineering expertise and*

experience gained from installing thousands of scoreboards to work at stadiums and ballparks across the globe.

From humble beginnings in 1968, Daktronics has grown to become a recognized leader worldwide in the programmable display industry. The company was started by two professors of electrical engineering. Daktronics, whose main strength is its design and engineering capability, is considered the "can-

The 1992 Summer Olympic Games, Barcelona, Spain.

do" company throughout the industry. Today it provides scoring systems for every sport at every level of competition. Its scoreboards and displays communicate with millions each and every day in 50 different countries on six continents. It's no wonder that stadium architects and facility managers look to Daktronics for unique solutions to the challenge of entertaining and informing fans and promoting events at their stadiums and ballparks.

VIDEO DISPLAYS, PROGRAMMABLE MATRIX BOARDS, AND FIXED-FORMAT SCOREBOARDS

Video displays, matrix boards, and fixed-format scoreboards are the three kinds of displays used in sports facilities. Large-screen video displays are popular but remain financially out of reach for all but the largest sports facilities.

Fixed-format scoreboards and full matrix boards are a necessity at larger sports facilities. Fixed-format scoreboards are dedicated to displaying game-in-progress information (scores, game time, etc.). In many facilities, matrix boards offer most of the features and excitement of video at a fraction of the cost.

Matrix boards are comprised of light-emitting or reflective pixels that are controlled by computer. These boards can display a myriad of information in many different character fonts and sizes. On a typical display, thousands of pixels are lighted or rotated to show text, graphics, and animation. Often used in conjunction with fixed-format scoreboards and video displays, matrix boards are especially popular. They can be used to display lineups, player and team information, as well as entertaining graphics and animation during breaks for fans. With Daktronics' Venus® 6000 control system and an operator who realizes the importance of his or her job, matrix boards add excitement and entertainment value at a game or other event. Matrix boards are also frequently used in front of a stadium or arena to promote upcoming events to those passing by. Monochrome, and 16, 256, and 65,536 color displays are available.

MATRIX BOARD TECHNOLOGIES

Matrix boards can be classified as light-emitting or reflective. Daktronics offers both kinds of technologies, for indoor and outdoor use. Patented Starburst® color and SunSpot® monochrome displays use incandescent lamps with unique reflectors and special lenses. Light-emitting displays offer high impact and faster changes (up to 30 frames per second). Daktronics' patented Glow Cube® technology employs rotating reflective pixels. Glow Cube® displays offer lower power and installation costs. Both types of displays provide excellent visibility and wide-angle viewing for spectators. Many different pixel/character sizes and hundreds of matrix configurations are available from Daktronics.

Oriole Park at Camden Yards, Baltimore, Maryland.

THE CONTROL SYSTEM

Daktronics has spent years developing and refining its Venus® 6000 control system for matrix board operation. The company uses the latest computer hardware available with its proprietary software. The software is designed with the operator in mind, making it easy to create and display text and graphic information. Easy-to-use drawing tools, coupled with the ability to capture video and still images, make creating graphics and animation easy. The controller's quick-display feature lets the scoreboard operator line up preprogrammed sequences for display in a split second.

DAKSTATS® STATISTICS SOFTWARE

Daktronics has developed its own software for recording and displaying game statistics. This unique software is integrated with the Venus® series controller, typically on a computer network, to show up-to-the-minute statistics. The DakStats® program for baseball has been a big hit at both Minor and Major League ballparks. The system allows the scoreboard operator to download statistics for both teams from Major League Baseball's mainframe computer prior to the start of the game, so fans see up-to-the-minute team and player stats. Then, when the game begins, the operator records each play on the computer, which updates the statistics throughout the game. Fans at the ballpark always get to see current statistics. (The computer screen pictured at right gives a better idea of how the program works.)

Daktronics has developed DakStats® software for many different sports as well. The programs have been used for golf, football, basketball, rodeo, figure skating, skiing, gymnastics, and weightlifting.

SCORES FROM AROUND THE COUNTRY

Daktronics has also developed the capability to display scores from other games around the country. The company takes advantage of satellite communications technology to receive information and display it immediately on the scoreboards. If you're watching the Orioles play the Indians at Camden Yards, for example, you can still keep track of other baseball action on a special scoreboard in right field that displays inning-by-inning scores and information of the action from other ballparks. Scores from other sports and activities can also be shown.

STATE-OF-THE-ART SCORING SYSTEMS FOR THE FUTURE

Over the past 25 years Daktronics has grown to become the leading scoreboard and programmable display manufacturer. The company takes pride in its ability to work closely with each individual sports facility to provide the scoring and display system that's just right. From the Kingdome in Seattle, to Oriole Park at Camden Yards; from Sydney, Australia, to Santiago, Chile, sports facilities count on Daktronics. The company will continue to take advantage of technological changes and develop new products and features to make going to the game even more fun.

A DakStats® Computer Screen.

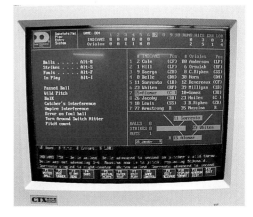

▶ Birdair, Inc.

Since its founding in 1956 by Walter Bird, Birdair, Inc., has been committed to maintaining international recognition as the world leader in the field of architectural membrane roofing systems. ✒ *Walter Bird is credited as the pioneer of air-supported "bubble" covers for swimming*

Right: Olympic Stadium, Rome, Italy. Architect: Italproggetti S.r.l. Roof Consultant: Studio Majowiecki. Photo by Robert Reck

Below: Georgia Dome, Atlanta, Georgia. Architects: Heery Architects & Engineers, Inc.; Rosser Fabrap International; Thompson Ventulett, Stainback & Associates, Inc. Engineer: Weidlinger Associates. Photo by Robert Reck

pools and tennis courts. Birdair, in conjunction with architects and engineers, advanced this technology to be applied toward long-span structures. This advanced technology gave an alternate solution to covering stadiums at a lower price with a longer life span. This application has been applied to the Pontiac Silverdome, Minneapolis Metrodome, Syracuse University Carrier Dome, Vancouver's B.C. Place, and the Indianapolis Hoosier Dome, in addition to various collegiate facilities.

In the 1980s Birdair participated in the development of the next generation of lightweight long-span roofing systems. These incorporated the use of cables and steel to create a tensegrity dome, and eliminated the need for an "air-supported" system. The first application was at the Redbird Arena for the University of Illinois. The structural system for this project was developed by David Geiger. This same applica-

tion was put to use on the ThunderDome in St. Petersburg, Florida. Weidlinger Associates of New York then developed another version of the cable dome, which Birdair installed in Atlanta on the Georgia Dome.

Although known primarily for "domed" stadiums, Birdair has also performed work on open-air stadiums, including the Olympic Stadium in Rome and the King Fahd International Stadium in Riyadh, Saudi Arabia. Stadiums such as these cover the spectator stands only, allowing for the growth of natural grass on the playing field.

Birdair continues to assist architects and engineers in creating the next generation of lightweight long-span roofing systems. This ranges from the development of retractable stadium roofs, to retro-

fitting existing facilities, to conventional metal deck roof systems that are half the weight of current steel stadium designs. Designers and engineers around the world credit Birdair with the application of SHEER-FILL Architectural Membrane, a Teflon-coated woven fiberglass, which has been used on all the air-

supported dome stadiums, as well as the Thunder-Dome and Georgia Dome. Birdair uses SHEERFILL on a variety of other structures, ranging from airports (the New Denver International Airport) to retail malls, amphitheaters, walkway covers, convention centers, and other public use facilities. It offers a life expectancy in excess of 20 years, light translucency, energy efficiency, and a dramatic visual signature statement.

The company also has used a variety of other lightweight materials such as glass, thin metal, and other flexible membranes. These options, coupled with numerous structural approaches, result in a variety of solutions and options for the client.

Birdair is a comprehensive resource that offers clients detail design and engineering support, construction management, cost budgeting, value engineering, and long-term customer service. Its employees continue to be energized by new concepts and challenges, resulting in the firm having a satisfied customer base throughout the world.

SHEERFILL Architectural Membrane is a registered trademark of Chemfab Corporation.

▶ Ellerbe Becket

Ellerbe Becket provides architectural and engineering design, planning, and construction management, design/build, and post-occupancy services to clients worldwide. Ellerbe Becket maintains offices in Kansas City, New York City, Washington, D.C., Minneapolis, and Los Angeles, which

collectively employ more than 800 staff members.

Today's complex building environment requires the combined services of many specialists to carry a project from concept to completion. As a single-source provider of total planning, design, and construction services, Ellerbe Becket is serving clients in the area of sports, leisure, and entertainment facilities—throughout the United States and worldwide. Through cohesive interdisciplinary groups that focus on specific client areas, Ellerbe Becket offers the stability and state-of-the-art resources of a large firm, combined with the creative atmosphere and personal attention of the small design studio.

SPORTS/LEISURE/ENTERTAINMENT EXPERTISE

Ellerbe Becket offers special expertise in the planning and design of sports, leisure, and entertainment facilities. We offer the combined experience and resources of personnel who have been involved in this specialized field for over 30 years. Our professional portfolio includes some of the latest and most successful complexes in the increasingly competitive entertainment industry.

Some of the firm's more notable projects include the 1996 Olympic Stadium, Atlanta, Georgia; the new Gund Arena in Cleveland, Ohio; Universal Studios, Orlando, Florida; the Rose Garden Arena Entertainment Complex, Portland, Oregon; the New CoreStates Center, Philadelphia, Pennsylvania; the MGM Grand Garden, Las Vegas, Nevada; the Fleet-Center, Boston, Massachusetts; the Retractable-Roof Baseball Stadium for the Major League expansion franchise in Phoenix, Arizona; and the new Sonas Center, a stadium/arena/entertainment complex in Dublin, Ireland.

Ellerbe Becket's professionals have the important technical knowledge and experience required to make these projects function correctly and efficiently, while expressing the unique flair of award-winning architecture with a reputation for state-of-the-art,

forward-thinking design concepts.

Ellerbe Becket understands the business and operations issues associated with sports/leisure/entertainment development. We have the technical skills required to provide owners, operators, promoters, concessionaires, and tenants with spaces that are designed to be functionally efficient, well-planned, and that allow maximum opportunities for revenue generation.

Our staff includes planners and urban designers who analyze long-range, broad-spectrum issues such as urban design and redevelopment, the planning of entire "Entertainment Districts" that promote redevelopment and create destination locations, as well as pedestrian and vehicular ingress and egress issues for frequent high-volume special events.

AWARD-WINNING EXPERIENCE

The Sports and Public Assembly Group of Ellerbe Becket has completed over 100 assignments in this specialized marketplace and has a national and international reputation for quality design, functional excellence, and delivery on-time and within budget. This group is proud to have been the recipient of numerous design awards from such prestigious sources as the American Institute of Architects, *Progressive Architecture* magazine, and *Athletic Business* magazine.

Above: Phoenix Major League Ballpark, Phoenix, Arizona.

Top: 1996 Olympic Stadium/Atlanta Braves Ballpark, Atlanta, Georgia.

► Krueger International

KI, founded in 1941 as Krueger Metal Products, is the nation's seventh-largest manufacturer of office, commercial, and institutional furniture, with sales of more than $280 million. ► *The company started manufacturing metal folding chairs in Aurora, Illinois, but corporate growth*

and new product development increased dramatically after a move to Green Bay in 1945. KI is now employee owned and synonymous with technically innovative, high-value products designed to meet customers' specific needs. A commitment to quality and total employee involvement puts KI at the forefront of leading-edge companies.

"KI is committed to satisfying the needs of our customers," states president and chief executive officer Dick Resch. "Our vision statement—'Improving Your Quality of Life'—is more than a cliché, it's the primary purpose behind our business."

Customer-focused and niche-marketing philosophies drive KI's growth, which recently has occurred at a rate more than four and one-half times faster than the industry average. Vertically integrated, with a cellular manufacturing arrangement, KI received the prestigious ISO 9000 registration for quality for all of its manufacturing facilities and corporate support functions.

KI targets products for stadiums and arenas, colleges and universities, hospitals, airports, restaurants, hotels, offices, corporate training environments, and malls. KI's products include office seating, stacking and guest chairs, tandem seating, systems furniture, tables, wall systems, and fiberglass site furnishings.

A number of KI's products were designed specifically for stadiums and arenas. KI remains the world's largest manufacturer of metal folding chairs with a variety of models and styles. Arena and stadium managers can choose from the standard metal folding chair to KI's Comfort Line®, Design Line®, and Logo Seating, which allows for sports team logos to be incorporated in the design of the chair. Piretti, Perry, and Matrix stack chairs provide alternatives of durability, style, and ergonomics. KI's Piretti and Vertebra seating make ideal choices for seating in stadium club seats or luxury boxes, which require superior aesthetics and comfort. Fiberglass planters and trash receptacles put the finishing touch on any athletic venue.

Historic Lambeau Field in Green Bay and the Georgia Dome in Atlanta are two stadiums using a cross-section of KI products. Vertebra seating in a variety of models is used throughout the luxury boxes at Lambeau Field. The state-of-the-art Georgia Dome relies on 10,000 of KI's durable and high-value 731 deluxe folding chairs.

KI and its employees are strong supporters of professional, college, high school, and youth athletic programs throughout the Green Bay metro area. Employees company-wide donate countless hours and resources to area charities including the YMCA, community zoo, the arts, domestic abuse shelters, and more.

With corporate headquarters and a manufacturing plant in Green Bay, KI also operates manufacturing facilities in Gillett and Manitowoc, Wisconsin; Tupelo and Winona, Mississippi; and Pembroke, Ontario, Canada. KI employs 2,300 people, with 725 people at its corporate office and Green Bay plant and about 1,100 in all of its Wisconsin operations.

Historic Lambeau Field in Green Bay uses KI Vertebra seating throughout the luxury boxes.

▶ Sony Electronics Inc.

SONY®

People are looking up to Sony ▬ *At 43rd and Broadway, you can*

catch them looking. They're looking in theme parks. In the NFL, the NBA, the

NHL, Major League Baseball, and the NCAA. People are lifting their faces

toward the Sony Jumbotron® Giant Screen Display. Famed for its brightness

and sharpness. Cheered for its contrast. Applauded for its reliability. Sony

Jumbotron Giant Screens. Next time you're in the neighborhood, look us up.

JumboTron

▶ Wrightson, Johnson, Haddon & Williams, Inc.

Imagine watching a baseball game without hearing the crack of the ball connecting against the bat, or seeing the offensive and defensive lines collide without hearing the hard-hitting crunch of football helmets.

The senses of sound and sight are vital elements of professional sports

entertainment. As spectator knowledge and appreciation of electronics and technology increases, so does the appreciation of stadium and ballpark sound and video systems and their broadcasts have become a distinguishing factor in the overall quality of a sporting facility. The challenge of stadium owners and managers, vying for precious entertainment market-share, is to satisfy increasingly sophisticated fans. Helping stadium owners and managers meet this challenge is the specialty of design firm Wrightson, Johnson, Haddon & Williams (WJHW).

Right: WJHW has done design and consulting work for The Ballpark in Arlington. ©1994 Glenn Patterson/SkyCam

Below: WJHW technical design innovations are in place at Hong Kong Stadium. Courtesy, HOK Sport

Principals Jack Wrightson, Jim Johnson, Bill Haddon, and Chris Williams and their staff specialize in the design of technical systems for stadiums and arenas. Typical design services provided by WJHW for a stadium include sound systems, scoreboard/video displays, TV and radio broadcast cabling, video replay production, specialized video survelliance, distributed TV, facility-wide low-voltage electronic system coordination, acoustics, and noise control. Also included in WJHW's expertise is the design, specification, and negotiation of scoreboard and large-scale video display systems.

Working as part of an architectural design team,

or directly with stadium owners or tenants, WJHW distinguishes itself as a design and consulting firm; it neither sells nor installs equipment, thus providing clients with appropriate, independent advice. Similar to the way an architect designs and specifies products best suited to the needs of a stadium project, WJHW offers strictly independent design and consulting services for both renovation and new construction projects.

When providing design information, the firm strongly believes in the programming concept, in which design must follow the functional, operational, and economic direction set by facility management and tenants. This process not only ensures that the end result meets the expectations and needs of the facility, but can also achieve innovative solutions. WJHW is proud to be part of the design teams on new stadiums for the Charlotte Panthers and the Jacksonville Jaguars; St. Louis' domed football stadium; and new arenas including the Duck Pond in Anaheim, the United Center in Chicago, New Boston Garden in Boston, Oregon Arena in Portland, and the Nashville Arena.

Among its accomplishments, WJHW has made design innovations in distributed loudspeaker systems that improve sound quality and allow superior synchronization of sound with video display systems. This sophisticated technology is in use at Candlestick Park, Busch Stadium, Comiskey Park, SkyDome, Oriole Park, Jacobs Field, and The Ballpark in Arlington.

As specialists in sports facilities, Wrightson, Johnson, Haddon & Williams is actively preparing for the future of sports entertainment systems, including interactive TV and scoring systems, and responding to the ongoing diversity of spectators and their expectations. While looking to the future, WJHW remains dedicated to old-fashioned principles of client service and responsiveness.

▶ Panasonic Broadcast and Television Systems Company

NEW PANASONIC DIVISION TO SELL LARGE-SCREEN VIDEO DISPLAYS TO STADIUM, ARENA, AND PUBLIC VENUE MARKETS

Panasonic's Astrovision, the high-brightness, high-resolution large-screen video display system, and Panasonic multiscreen video cube systems are leading-edge video displays ideal for indoor and outdoor applications,

including sports stadiums, indoor arenas, multipurpose halls, amusement parks, airports and train and bus stations, building exteriors, video billboards, stores and shopping malls, museums and galleries, and car, dog, and horse racing tracks.

Panasonic Astrovision displays feature Fluorescent Discharge Tube technology that allows for high brightness, high-resolution color reproduction, long life, and easy maintenance. Panasonic markets three series of Astrovision displays: AZ-1400 (with 14mm pitch) for indoor use, and the AZ-1600 (with 18mm pitch) and AZ-3000 (with 30mm pitch) for indoor and outdoor applications. The displays' brightness is more than 5000 nit (cd/m2), which enables the installation of Astrovision in various lighting conditions. More than 100 Astrovision displays have been installed worldwide. Panasonic will customize the display to the size the customer requires.

A Panasonic video cube system incorporates high-brightness 43-inch video cubes that can work as a stand-alone display or be stacked to form a multiscreen system. With 600-lumen output and outstanding horizontal resolution of 1,000 lines for RGB and 800 lines for video, images produced by the 43-inch cubes are breathtakingly bright and sharp when viewed from a distance or close up.

To create a turnkey audio/video system, Panasonic can supply a broad range of products including broadcast and professional VTRs, cameras, monitors, editing systems, projectors, Ramsa professional audio products, optical memory video disc recorders and players, laser disc players, videoconferencing systems, security systems, and other video equipment.

For more information on Panasonic large-screen video displays and related products, call 201/392-6591.

Panasonic Astrovision displays feature Fluorescent Discharge Tube technology that allows for high brightness, high-resolution color reproduction, long life, and easy maintenance.

▶ Freudenberg Building Systems, Inc.

For more than 45 years Freudenberg has been making its Nora Rubber Flooring, synonymous with quality, and Freudenberg Building Systems, Inc.—the American branch—has relied on its R&D facilities to constantly refine the Nora rubber flooring technology and to develop solutions for

For high style and performance off the ice, Pan Am Ice Skating Rink, Indianapolis, Indiana, uses Norament 992 S in a warm red pastille-type application.

the toughest floor covering problems. It is part of the multinational Freudenberg Group, founded in 1849, which employs 26,000 people worldwide and has over 20 facilities in the United States.

Today Norament and Noraplan flooring systems are best known for their quality and variety. They come in more styles and colors and meet more performance criteria for extremely heavy to normal traffic conditions than any other rubber flooring in the world. Also, unique products are created to meet design and functional requirements for special applications. Supported by the expertise of Nora technical advisors and sales staff, Freudenberg Building Systems now ranks number one in sales and performance worldwide.

Used in demandingly high-traffic environments, installations of Nora rubber flooring can be found in many stadiums and sports facilities in the United States and abroad. Norament products—with raised circles and squares and a coned back—withstand the stress of heavy traffic and even the extra abuse of forklifts, are specially formulated for low maintenance costs, and are extremely resistant to cuts, punctures, and tears.

Freudenberg Building Systems, Inc., anticipates continued growth based on the satisfaction of end-users and stadium owners as it moves into the twenty-first century equipped with quality products that promise to be as competitive as they are colorful.

Right: This minor-league ballpark is located near the water's edge in St. Petersburg, Florida. Photo by James Blank / Scenics of America

Facing page: University of Virginia Cheerleaders at Scott Stadium. Photo by Daniel Grogan

*U*niversity of Nebraska fans arrive on game day dressed in red from head to toe; some even paint their faces and hands red. In fact, attend a UN game in Lincoln and you're bound to see about 75,000 fans wearing red. Courtesy, Nebraska Sports Information

FAN TRADITIONS

From Tailgating to Twelfth Men

When a visiting player hits a home run against the Chicago Cubs in Wrigley Field, the fan who retrieves the ball is tradition bound to throw it back onto the field. When the visiting team scores a touchdown at Michigan Stadium in Ann Arbor, Michigan student fans in the north end zone stands pelt the field with marshmallows. Fraternity members at the University of Virginia and University of Alabama wear ties and jackets to home football games in Charlottesville and Tuscaloosa. At Kyle Field at College Station, Texas, Texas A&M fans stand through every minute of every home game, honoring the legend, begun in 1922, of the "Twelfth Man." In Columbia, South Carolina, University of South Carolina Gamecocks fans

tailgate outside Williams-Brice Stadium in "cockabooses." And in a demonstration of whimsy characteristic of San Francisco, fans who stay until the end of extra-inning night games at Candlestick Park are awarded lapel pins known as the Croix de Candlestick.

Welcome to the world of fan traditions, the rituals that enrich and enliven the stadium-going experience. With long-standing customs such as throwing back an opponent's home run ball at Wrigley Field, fans give stadium and team their individuality, character, and continuity. Traditions add to the luster of championship seasons; they also help console fans during losing campaigns and provide the strength to wait till next year.

Harking back to the Roman Colosseum, where spectators determined whether a fallen gladiator lived or died by turning their collective thumbs up or down, fan traditions come in shapes and sizes to fit all occasions.

Some fan traditions are institutionalized in legendary sports rivalries. Indiana and Purdue have been vying for the Old Oaken Bucket since 1925 in one of college football's most colorful rivalries; after each game, the bucket is painted with a "P" or "I", depending on who won the game. Michigan and Minnesota have been competing for the Little Brown Jug, originally a 30-cent water bottle, since 1903. DePauw University and Wabash College play for the Monon Bell, an old train bell from the Monon Railroad, which ran between the two Indiana schools. The University of Washington and Washington State compete for the Apple Cup. And on and on.

Some traditions just kind of happen, such as the fan migration from the aluminum bleachers of the University of Virginia's Scott Stadium to the more relaxed atmosphere of "the hill," an earthen embankment behind

the north end zone, as the game progresses. In Starkville, Mississippi, Mississippi State students like to gather for refreshments in their baseball stadium's "left field lounge."

We also have what could be called copy-cat traditions. For example, student fans throw marshmallows at opposing teams at Bucknell, Penn State, and Northwestern as well as at Michigan. University of Pennsylvania fans have a variation on the theme; after singing "Here's a toast to dear old Penn," they throw toast on the field.

Fan traditions have their comedic side. The San Diego Chicken has been cavorting around San Diego Jack Murphy Stadium for decades. The Hogettes, a group of beefy, male Washington Redskins fans who began donning pig

snouts and outlandish dresses in honor of the Skins' offensive line back in 1983, have become an institution at Robert F. Kennedy Memorial Stadium and throughout the Washington, D.C., area. Go back to the glory days of Ebbets Field for memories of the Brooklyn Dodgers Sym-phony, a group of ardent Dodger fans who banged cymbals and bass drums, blew whistles and kazoos, and ended up being as much a part of Dodger lore as Jackie, Campy, and the Duke. Not to be outdone, Boston (now Milwaukee) Braves fans formed their own version of the Sym-phony, calling themselves the Boston

Facing page: Shirts and ties are still the traditional garb for some University of Virginia students watching home games at Scott Stadium. Photo by Daniel Grogan

Green Bay Packer fans have turned tailgating into a fine art in the Lambeau Field parking lot. Pictured here before a game are Mike and Mary Gerrits of Green Bay and Larry and Kay Mercier of De Pere, Wisconsin. Courtesy, America's Pack Fan Club

12TH MAN

Above: Texas A&M started the "Twelfth Man" tradition on New Year's Day of 1922; and to this day, throughout every home game, Aggie fans stand to honor the original twelfth man—E. King Gill. Courtesy, Texas A&M

Right: On Lake Washington, some fans of the University of Washington Huskies engage in aquatic tailgating near Husky Stadium. The popularity of this pregame event has led to a 10-year waiting list for mooring spaces. Courtesy, University of Washington

Troubadours. Fan bands extend beyond baseball. Clemson University made the *Guinness Book of World Records* for having the largest kazoo band at a sporting event.

Marching bands, with their operatic uniforms and spectacularly intricate halftime maneuvers, are a tradition unto themselves. The bands of the Big Ten, the Southeastern Conference, and the historically black colleges (Florida A&M University's band is world famous) week after week perform prodigious feats of athleticism and musicianship. In pregame ceremonies at Baton Rouge, Louisiana, the Louisiana State band marches into the end zone of Tiger Stadium and whips fans into a frenzy by playing "Fight for LSU" four times, once in each direction. Some bands are notable for other reasons. The Yale band once mooned the fans in Yale Bowl. The marching band of The College of Wooster (in

Ohio) takes to the field in Scottish kilts at halftime for what is considered the highlight of the game.

Fan traditions are also fashions like the wave, said to have originated in Dodger Stadium, in which successive sections of spectators rise from their seats and languidly wave both arms above their heads; in certain West Coast ballparks, a well-timed wave in the stands draws louder applause than a grand slam homer or a triple play on the field. Today's most prevalent fan tradition/fashion by far is the tailgate party, which began on the sedate greenswards outside Ivy League playing fields and now ranks with Thanksgiving dinner as an American gustatory institution and media event.

Taking a closer look at some of the more familiar and colorful fan traditions:

The Twelfth Man. This has become the generic designation for any external factor—a blizzard, the deafening roar of partisan fans—that helps a home team win a football game. There actually was a game, back on New Year's Day of 1922, where the twelfth man was a critical factor. He even had a name: E. King Gill. Texas A&M was hosting Centre College, a small Kentucky college with an undefeated football team, at the Dixie classic in what is now the Cotton Bowl in Dallas. It was a hard-fought game, and injuries soon depleted the Aggies' total strength down to the bare minimum of 11 men. (Teams played both ways in those days.) It was then that the Aggies' coach remembered that E. King Gill, a sophomore football player who had been released from the postseason game to join the basketball team, was working as a spotter in the stadium. The coach yanked Gill away from his spotting duties, handed him a uniform, and told him to put it on, giving the Aggies a substitute in case of another injury. Gill—Texas A&M's twelfth man—never entered the game, but by merely standing on the sideline, he inspired the Aggies to a 22-14 upset victory. To this day, Texas A&M fans stand throughout every home game to honor E. King Gill, the original twelfth man—and to be ready to jump into the game just in case.

Throwing them back at Wrigley Field.

Wrigley Field, one of the few original urban ballparks (it was built in 1914), is a reservoir of traditions. One of the best known is that of tossing a home run ball hit by a visiting player back on to the field. Why? Because, the story goes, if a Cub didn't hit the homer, the ball wasn't worth keeping. The unwritten throw-back rule extends from the spectators in the stands to the ball hawks outside the stadium on Waveland and Sheffield avenues. The tradition is said to have originated in the 1960s with the Bleacher Bums, a raffish, ad hoc group of fans who inhabited Wrigley's cheap outfield seats. Local folklore has it that the Bleacher Bums offered to compensate anyone who threw back the opponent's home run ball with a beer. Another time-honored

fan tradition at Wrigley: Singing along with gravel-voiced play-by-play announcer Harry Carey as he belts out "Take Me Out to the Ball Game" on the public address system during the seventh-inning stretch.

Tailgating, the new national pastime. If you think it's tough getting a seat in some stadiums, try finding a place to tailgate outside a stadium. After beginning modestly as pregame picnic lunches served off the lowered rear doors of station wagons, tailgating has grown into a national institution. Whether the venue is a high school, college, or NFL stadium, the three hours before kick-

off are dedicated to eating and partying in the parking lot. The first rule of tailgating is that you don't need a tailgate *per se.* Fans routinely set up tables and chairs and cook on charcoal grills. It is not unusual to see fans pulling into stadium parking lots before dawn to begin roasting a turkey or suckling pig. By midmorning, clouds of charcoal smoke ring the stadium like a suet-scented mist. At big college football weekends, such as those in the Big Ten, vans and RVs begin filling stadium parking lots and surrounding fields on Friday nights and stay through Sunday.

About 7,000 members of the 13,000-strong America's Pack Fan Club take over a fenced-in area of Lambeau Field for a three-hour tailgate party featuring food, drink, and entertainment. Courtesy, America's Pack Fan Club

Left: Bratwurst is the food of choice at Lambeau Field's tailgate parties. Courtesy, America's Pack Fan Club

Right and below:
Refurbished freight train
cabooses purchased by
local businesses and
outfitted with all the
amenities of a well-
appointed living room
comprise the
Cockaboose Railroad at
the University of South
Carolina. The
cockabooses provide a
genteel alternative to the
parking lot tailgate
party. Photos by Jeff
Salter. Courtesy,
University of South
Carolina Sports
Information

season for access to the three-hour party that provides bratwurst (or "brats"), beer, and name entertainment for up to 7,000 fans at each home game. Retired Packer players from the Lombardi era regale the crowd with war stories. At least one America's Pack tailgate party featured a sumo wrestling match. America's Pack Fan Club members migrate to Tampa for the Tampa Bay Buccaneers-Packers game and, at an estimated 5,000 people, for what they claim to be America's biggest tailgate party.

Some other examples of how far tailgating has come:

- Two major college stadiums are the scene of what can only be called aquatic tailgating. The University of Tennessee's Neyland Stadium, on the Tennessee River, and the University of Washington's Husky Stadium, by Lake Washington, are the scene of waterborne tailgate parties. Both schools have built dockage areas for the boats since the practice began. Tailgating at Lake Washington, outside Seattle, has become so popular that there is a 10-year waiting list for mooring spaces.

- In Green Bay, Wisconsin, the America's Pack Fan Club, a national organization of 13,000 Green Bay Packers fans, has a large, fenced-in area of the Lambeau Field parking lot designated as its tailgate party area. Members pay anywhere from $30 to $65 per

- For the tailgater who has seen it all or wants it all, a group of well-heeled University of South Carolina Gamecocks football fans presents the "Cockaboose Railroad." Located on a railroad track behind the University's Williams-Brice Stadium, the Cockaboose Railroad consists of 22 old freight train cabooses purchased by local businesses and fitted out with running water, cable television, air conditioning and heating, and luxurious appointments and furnishings. Cockabooses cost upwards of $100,000 and don't go anywhere even though they're on a railroad siding. But for the tailgater who prefers to enjoy a pre-kick-off snack and beverage sheltered from the elements and away from the crowd, the cockaboose is just the ticket.

The Brooklyn Dodgers Sym-phony. Their sound would have made Toscanini cringe, yet they serenaded dignitaries like President Dwight Eisenhower and baseball magnate Connie Mack and the era's most glámorous couple, Humphrey Bogart and Lauren Bacall, all in Section 8 of Ebbets Field. They were the Dodgers Sym-phony (with a self-imposed emphasis on *phony*), a bunch of zealous Bums fans from the Greenpoint section of Brooklyn who got together in 1937 to have a good time making noise with improvised musical instruments. They achieved national fame during the 1940s and 1950s, when the Dodgers were America's team and Ebbets Field and its denizens were beloved for their zaniness. While an occasional legitimate musician might sneak in, the seven-member Sym-phony's typical instrumentation was a police whistle, bass drum, cymbals, megaphone, kazoo, and maybe a bugle. The group's basic repertoire included: "Three Blind Mice," played when the umpires took the field; "Give Me Five Minutes More," played when a manager was about to yank a pitcher; "Somebody Else is Taking My Place," when a visiting pitcher was relieved; and "How Dry I Am," played whenever a visiting player went to the water fountain. Founded and led by a transit worker named Jack "Shorty" Laurice, the Symphony eventually received the official sanction of the Dodger organization and formed familial relationships. They attended each other's weddings, christenings, and funerals with such Dodger immortals as Jackie Robinson, Roy Campanella, Carl Erskine, and Pee Wee Reese. The fans were also in on the act; they gave Shorty a day of his own in Ebbets Field. Today fabric sculptures of Shorty Laurice and two of his sidemen grace an exhibit devoted to fans at the Baseball Hall of Fame in Cooperstown. You can see them playing, but you can't hear them (which may not be a bad thing).

The Hogettes, the sweethearts of RFK. Their motto is "Ugly is skin deep" and their favorite designer is "Calvin Swine." They go to Washington Redskins football games in outlandish dresses, fright wigs, army boots, and rubber pig snouts. They are the Hogettes, and since 1983 they have been the primo cheering section for the Skins' offensive line, dubbed the Hogs. Take away their costumes and you have about a dozen big, beefy guys who are family

men and who share a fanatical commitment to the Redskins. Says Mike Torbert, the Boss Hogette: "The offensive line is made up of no-name players, so we felt they deserved their own cheerleading squad." Like the Dodgers Sym-phony at Ebbets Field, the Hogettes occupied the same section for every home game at Robert F. Kennedy Memorial Stadium and first attracted media notice when reporters spotted pin-up pictures of the Hogettes in the Redskins' locker room. The Hogettes have appeared in a Ford commercial and earned an honorary place on commentator John Madden's All-Madden team. Also, they have parlayed their fame into a force for good, making 100 personal appearances a year in bowling tournaments, golf tournaments, even polo matches, to raise

Since their formation in 1983, the outrageous Hogettes, the sweethearts of Robert F. Kennedy Memorial Stadium, have helped raise more than $50 million to aid Washington, D.C.-area children. Courtesy, Mike Torbert

funds for children's charities and visiting sick and terminally ill children. Since their formation, the Hogettes have helped raise $50 million to aid children in the Washington, D.C., area. "We love to make kids laugh," says Torbert, citing the Hogette motto: "A child's smile is a great joy," and leaving with the Hogette benediction: "May cool slop be with you always."

*T*he Seattle Kingdome, home to the Seattle Seahawks and the Seattle Mariners, hosts a multitude of other events as well. Courtesy, Seattle Kingdome

MULTIUSE STADIUMS

Versatile Venues

It used to be that a stadium was a stadium was a stadium, but this is no longer the case. Today stadiums can be changed from the surface to the dome to suit an infinite variety of tenants, events, and uses. Let fans and media heap accolades—all richly deserved—on the retro-genre, baseball-only ballparks that ushered in the 1990s. Many believe, however, that the true wave of the future lies in technologically advanced, fan-friendly, image-burnishing multipurpose stadiums and event environments.

This premise rests on three pillars. First, most of today's new stadiums are financed by taxpayers and, therefore, must be considered a public resource available for uses ranging from big-league football and

Cincinnati Riverfront
Stadium, built next to
the Ohio River in 1970,
was designed to house
both baseball and
football teams. Photo by
James Blank / Scenics of
America

baseball to conventions and concerts to religious revivals and junior high school volleyball. Second, imposing, versatile, conveniently located stadium complexes are symbols of civic pride and accomplishment. Finally, because building a stadium costs upwards of $150 million or more and maintaining one requires an annual outlay in the millions, a steady stream of events is necessary to provide the cash flow to pay the facility's mortgage and to keep its seats, concourses, concessions, rest rooms, and playing field in top shape.

Virtually every stadium is at some time or another multipurpose, even those strongly identified with a single sport. Texas Stadium, synonymous with football and the Dallas Cowboys, draws its biggest crowds when Garth Brooks puts on his country and western music extravaganzas. Cleveland Stadium, now the exclusive turf of the NFL's Browns, was once home to the Cleveland Indians as well as the venue for events ranging from midget auto racing to grand opera. Yankee Stadium, eternally famous for the New York

The Astrodome was the first domed stadium when it opened in 1965. This photo features the Astros against the Pirates. Photo by Scott Berner / The Stockhouse Inc., Houston

Yankees, has also hosted heavyweight championship fights, big-name college and pro football games, and a Papal visit. Tampa Stadium, famous for its award-winning natural turf, will host annual tractor pulls and Supercross events.

Stadiums designed, constructed, and promoted on a principle of maximum utilization eventually have become a category unto themselves. The new generation of stadiums has brought with it new technologies and materials, notably domes and artificial turf.

The stadiums built during the 1960s and 1970s (Cincinnati Riverfront Stadium and Pittsburgh's Three Rivers Stadium, to name two) were designed to house both baseball and football teams. Rock concerts, motor sports, and fireworks displays, among other events, were sought after to fill stadiums' rev-

The City of Indianapolis built the Hoosier Dome, now named the RCA Dome, as an expansion to the Indiana Convention Center in 1984. The NFL's Indianapolis Colts call this 60,500-seat venue home. Photo by Banayote. Courtesy, ICVA

enue gaps when the baseball and football teams were idle or traveling.

The latest entry in the multiple-use category is The Domed Stadium at America's Center in St. Louis. The 70,000-seat Domed Stadium, now home to the St. Louis (nee Los Angeles) Rams, opened in October 1995 as the crown jewel of the city's six-building multipurpose convention center and sports complex. Until their move to St. Louis, the Rams had played in the cavernous Los Angeles Memorial Coliseum (1946-1979) and the aging and earthquake-damaged Anaheim Stadium (1980-1994).

Built by the St. Louis Regional Convention & Sports Complex Authority for about $260 million, The Domed Stadium epitomizes today's multipurpose facility. Not only the home field to an NFL team, the stadium

serves the additional purpose of being a major-league convention, exhibition, and cultural center. Lawrence Akley, the Authority's executive director, says that even without an NFL or other big-time sports franchise, the stadium, with its 1.7 million square feet, 180-foot-high steel-trussed roof, and four-section moveable light grid, still would have been a busy trade show, concert, and convention site.

The stadium, which adjoins the five-building Cervantes Convention Center, also offers nearly 100,000 square feet of meeting and hospitality space at its suite and club levels. Its kitchen facilities can lay on a banquet for as many as 8,000 people. Concert rigging in the roof structure can support five stage or platform configurations weighing 100,000 pounds or more. An advanced system of air

(Text continues on page 67)

Who Uses Stadiums?

On a chill Toronto night in late November 1994, more than 10,000 "Beaver" scouts, ages 5 to 7, slept on a stadium field a block from wind-whipped Lake Ontario. It was a different experience for the scouts, but hardly an exercise in the rigors of outdoor survival. The boys' overnight, which commemorated the 20th anniversary of the Beavers in Canadian scouting, took place in Toronto's celebrated and versatile SkyDome. Their sleeping bags were spread on padded Astroturf, and the youngsters were sheltered by eight acres of steel-trussed roof. To help lull them to sleep, a bedtime story was shown on the 33-foot by 110-foot Sony JumboTron®, the world's largest video display board.

The Beaver Scout overnight event, unique for even as busy and eclectic a venue as SkyDome, symbolizes the increasing use of stadiums by a lengthening list and growing variety of organizations and attractions. Professional, college, and scholastic football, baseball, and soccer teams only top the list of stadium users.

Concert promoters, community organizations, evangelists, and car salesmen, to name a few, use stadiums with growing frequency. In the case of SkyDome, the number of days the stadium hosts events other than Blue Jays baseball or Argonauts football games increased from 165 in 1990 to 250 in 1993. Whether talking about Liza Minelli or monster trucks, Madonna or MotoCross, Pink Floyd or Billy Graham, no venue can match a stadium when it comes to hosting a major event.

With their capacity to seat more than 40,000 people, park upwards of 20,000 cars, and their built-in ability to provide lighting and amplification, handle and store equipment and sets, mount immense video screens, change surfaces and configurations, and feed tens of thousands of people, stadiums are in a class by themselves as showplaces. Domed stadiums have the added advantages of protecting against the weather and being able to curtain off sections to accommo-

Elton John, Billy Joel, and the Rolling Stones have all performed at Robert F. Kennedy Stadium in Washington, D.C.

COURTESY, DISTRICT OF COLUMBIA SPORTS COMMISSION / ROBERT F. KENNEDY MEMORIAL STADIUM

date arena-sized crowds and events.

The world's biggest and most popular acts know this and gear up for stadium tours that can draw upwards of 3 million fans and reach grosses of $100 million. Ben Liss, executive director of the MacLean, Virginia-based North American Concert Promoters Association, points out that stadium tours are important to performers for three basic reasons: "They help the act build a fan base; they help a performer sustain a career over the long haul even as album sales diminish; and, because of their large seating capacity, stadiums satisfy pent-up fan demand."

Says Randy Levy of the Minneapolis concert promotion firm Rose Presents:

When an act plays a stadium, everything—the stage, the lighting, the sound system, the video display—has to be in proportion to its surroundings. Elton John and Billy Joel use industrial strength hydraulic lifts under their pianos in their stadium shows. The stages for Pink Floyd or the Rolling Stones are five stories high, but nobody notices because they're in proportion to the rest of the environment.

A closer look at the Rolling Stones' five-month Voodoo Lounge tour that hit 34 North American stadiums for one- to four-night stands reveals just what a stadium performance by a headline act involves. Start with people—250 of them on the road to support four performers. Add a stage measuring 220 feet by 85 feet by 92 feet that takes four days to construct and requires three different steel crews to move ahead of the tour and begin assembling stages in preparation for the next show. The tour also includes the world's largest mobile JumboTron® video replay screen, a 1.5-million-watt sound system, generators capable of putting out 4 million watts of power, 56 trailer trucks, nine custom-fitted buses, a custom-fitted Boeing 727, and, at the insistence of the FAA, aircraft warning lights placed on top of the stage.

According to Randy Levy of Rose Presents:

When you have a heavy-duty act like the Stones coming into a stadium, their people do everything from selling tickets and providing security to managing the lighting, sound, and special effects. All that's expected of the stadium is that it should be clean, lit, heated, and well-maintained.

Brian O'Donovan, manager of Foxboro Stadium near Boston (a stop on the Rolling Stones and Pink Floyd tours), says the stadium's job is crowd management, "which translates into getting people into the facility as quickly as possible and then out equally as quickly."

Motor sports promoters have found stadiums ideal venues for events such as motorcycle races and monster truck exhibitions. Such is the growing popularity of motor sports as stadium events that some stadiums report that these attractions can generate 35 percent of a stadium's net annual income *in just one month.*

"We use stadiums to simulate the open road environment in comfort for off-road motorcycle racing fans," says Rick Miller, president of Mickey Thompson Entertainment

A motorcycle racer speeds by spectators inside the Astrodome.

PHOTO BY ALAN MONTGOMERY / THE STOCKHOUSE INC., HOUSTON

Group of Anaheim, California. The Mickey Thompson race series, which is extending its tour from the West Coast to as far east as the RCA Dome in Indianapolis, features off-road MotoCross (Motorcycle) races as well as SuperCross events that feature higher jumps and bigger bikes.

Like rock concerts, motor sports involve changes to the stadium. Says Mickey Thompson's Rick Miller, "We put layers of plastic and plywood on the stadium floor, and then drive in dump trucks to apply the 9,000 or so cubic yards of dirt that will make up the race course." When the event is over, the dirt is trucked back out. Miller adds that the indoor stadiums on the Thompson tour have sufficient ventilation and that all the stadiums have tunnels large enough to allow trucks easy access.

Evangelical organizations such as Jehovah's Witnesses and the Billy Graham Crusade have been stadium mainstays for decades. Harvest Crusade, a relative newcomer, has based a successful growth strategy on stadium revivals. In addition, both Yankee Stadium and Giants Stadium have

played host to Papal visits.

Trade and consumer expositions such as sportsmen's expos and home and hospitality shows are a stadium staple. In some cases the events take place just outside the stadium. Wayne Brubaker, who heads a San Diego advertising and promotion agency bearing his name, produces auto and recreational vehicle sales events in stadium parking lots up and down the West Coast for local and regional groups of car dealers. The events, which Brubaker has been staging since 1982, last from 3 to 10 days.

As Brubaker states:

We chose stadiums for these off-site promotions for several reasons. First, stadiums have huge parking lots, with the parking spaces already marked. The dealers might put anywhere from 300 to 1,000 RV's and cars in the lot, leaving ample room for customers to park their cars. And everyone knows how to get to the Kingdome or Jack Murphy Stadium or wherever we're holding a sale, so we don't have to give directions. As they say in real estate, it's all location, location, location.

Left: Open-air, grass-surfaced Joe Robbie Stadium in Miami can be transformed from a football to baseball stadium (or vice versa) in only 12 hours. Photo by Dave Cross

Facing page: Minneapolis' Hubert H. Humphrey Metrodome is home to the Minnesota Twins, Minnesota Vikings, and University of Minnesota Golden Gophers football team. Photo by James Blank / Scenics of America

exchangers clears the exhaust fumes generated by motor sports events and by trucks making deliveries at the facility's seven loading docks. In addition, a two-story press box atop the stadium's seating area will accommodate sportswriters covering a ball game or pundits pontificating at a political convention.

The Domed Stadium is the latest in a generation of well-known and busy indoor and outdoor multipurpose stadiums. Some better-known examples:

- The *Indiana Convention Center and RCA Dome* in downtown Indianapolis. Opened in 1984, the 60,500-seat RCA Dome, home to the NFL's Indianapolis Colts, was the model for the St. Louis stadium-convention center project. Like the new St. Louis facility, the RCA Dome (renamed from Hoosier Dome in 1994) was built by the City of Indianapolis as an expansion to a convention center rather than as a stand-alone sports venue. Also, like its St. Louis counterpart, the RCA Dome got its impetus from an NFL franchise seeking greener pastures (the then Baltimore Colts).
- The *Astrodome USA,* granddaddy of them all, opened for business in 1965. A folklore

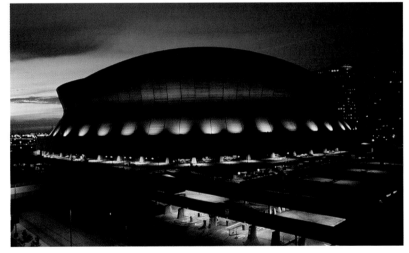

has developed around the Astrodome (also known as Harris County Domed Stadium and "The Eighth Wonder of the World"). It is the home of Astroturf, the artificial playing surface put into use when the original grass surface died because not enough sunlight filtered through the dome to nourish the sod. The Astrodome is the only domed stadium known to have had a game declared a rain out. This occurred when water from a flooded street spilled onto the playing field. On another occasion, the New York Mets protested, vainly, that the stadium staff was manipulating air currents to favor the bats

Above: The Louisiana Superdome takes on the appearance of a UFO in this nighttime shot. The New Orleans Saints play their home games here, and the facility hosts a number of other sporting events. The Superdome's soundproof rooms, which adjoin the playing field, accommodate many other events. Courtesy, Louisiana Superdome

Boat, auto, and recreational vehicle manufacturers and dealers have found stadiums—with their ample room and huge parking lots—to be the perfect venue for showcasing their products. Courtesy, Seattle Kingdome

of the home team Astros.

• Toronto's *SkyDome,* notable for having North America's first fully retractable roof and on-site luxury hotel, opened in 1989 and hosts baseball's Toronto Blue Jays and the Toronto Argonauts of the Canadian Football League. Calling itself the "World's Greatest Entertainment Centre," SkyDome has had, in the space of a month, an auto-mobile show, a circus, an indoor spring car-nival, the Harlem Globetrotters, and two pre-season Blue Jays games. At more than $400 million, SkyDome is North America's most expensive stadium.

• The *Louisiana Superdome,* in operation since 1975, is home to the New Orleans Saints of the NFL, the USF&G Sugar Bowl, Tulane football, and a procession of college football, baseball, and basketball tourna-ments. Four Super Bowls have been played there on artificial turf waggishly called "Mardi Grass." The Superdome's multipur-

pose nature is emphasized by four sound-proofed "quadrant" rooms adjoining the playing field that insulate sedate events such as crafts fairs and antique shows from the din of 62,000 howling football fans.

• The *Hubert H. Humphrey Metrodome* is the 64,000-seat Minneapolis home of the Min-nesota Twins, Minnesota Vikings, and the University of Minnesota Golden Gophers football team. It also welcomes inline skaters, runners, and corporate softball and volleyball teams at bargain rates. Baseball and football teams from high schools and small colleges around the state are no strangers to the Metrodome, which has hosted as many as 60 college baseball games in one month and was the scene of 10 col-lege football games in two days. In 1991, 72 high school football teams competing in the state playoffs played around the clock. Says Metrodome Director of Operations Dennis Alfton, "We're a publicly owned facility, so we should be more than a TV studio for pro sports."

- Seattle's *Kingdome,* opened in 1976, is versatility personified. In addition to being the home field of the Seahawks (football) and Mariners (baseball), the Kingdome has played host to the following: professional and international soccer matches, rodeos, NBA basketball, horse shows, antique shows, religious crusades, political rallies, college basketball and baseball, international volleyball tournaments, big-name rock concerts, circuses, motor sports, and paper airplane contests among many others.

125 events a year, the busiest grass-surfaced stadium in the United States. Home to the baseball Padres, the NFL Chargers, and the San Diego State football team, Jack Murphy also attracts more than its share of events such as national religious revivals, crafts shows, and tractor pulls inside the park. Even when the stadium itself is dark, Jack Murphy's parking lot is the scene of revenue-producing events—recreational vehicle shows, car sales, and auto races (to name just three). In the early fall, when baseball and football overlap, Jack Murphy reconfigures from baseball seating to football

Seattle's Kingdome hosts a variety of events ranging from professional and college sporting events to religious crusades and political rallies. Photo by James Blank / Scenics of America

- The *ThunderDome of St. Petersburg* advertises itself as "a multipurpose stadium that can accommodate virtually any kind of event." It also boasts that it was built primarily for major-league baseball and has hosted virtually every kind of spectator event—except baseball. A partial listing of events includes: Davis Cup Tennis, arena football, NHL hockey, NBA basketball, NCAA basketball (ThunderDome will be the venue for the 1999 Final Four), the AAU Junior Olympic games, trade and crafts shows, and a number of vehicular shows.
- *San Diego Jack Murphy Stadium* is, with

seating, only to return to baseball—all within fewer than three days.

- *Joe Robbie Stadium,* a privately financed, open-air, grass-surfaced facility built in 1987 for the Miami Dolphins and put through an $8-million renovation in 1994, was strictly a football stadium until the Florida Marlins, a National League expansion franchise, took the field in 1993. Unlike stadiums of the past, which were built for either football or baseball, but not both, Joe Robbie can do a complete and seamless makeover from football to baseball (or vice versa) in 12 hours. Retractable seating sections allow

The Ultimate Multiuse Challenge—World Cup Soccer

1994 will be remembered as the year the World Cup, soccer's Super Bowl, World Series, and Final Four wrapped into one, was played in stadiums designed and built for every game but soccer.

For the first time in its history, the World Cup tournament—with teams representing Italy, Rumania, Ireland, Germany, and Bulgaria—was coming to the United States to be played in stadiums built for American football, whose practitioners regard soccer as little more than a training ground for placekickers.

Two of the nine stadiums selected for the World Cup—Giants Stadium and the Pontiac Silverdome—have artificial surfaces and, therefore, posed a big problem: The International Soccer Federation, which sponsors the World Cup tournament, requires that games be played on natural surfaces.

The solution for both facilities was to grow natural turf over their artificial turf surfaces. The Silverdome grew 2,000 pieces of perennial rye and Kentucky bluegrass in its parking lot after attempts to grow a strong bed of grass in the filtered sunlight of the dome failed. Giants Stadium grew Bermuda grass in 5,400 tons of soil laid atop its artificial turf surface. Natural turf fans who hoped the grass would stay were disappointed. Both stadiums reverted to artificial turf when the World Cup competition ended. Explained Bill Squires, manager of Giants Stadium, "We play 30 pro and college football games a year here. The only kind of turf that can take that kind of beating is artificial."

spectator capacity to change from 75,000 (for football) to 47,000 (for baseball). Other modifications include a baseball press box, baseball dugouts, 660 additional lights for night baseball, a synthetic warning track that absorbs water, and a pitcher's mound that disappears under the ground electrically. Other events: NCAA bowl games, international soccer matches, motor sports races and rallies, and big-name concerts.

- *Aloha Stadium* in Honolulu, site of the Pro Bowl game, could be one of America's busiest facilities. With 50,000 seats, a low-maintenance artificial surface, and year-round good weather, Aloha Stadium is almost as much of an Hawaiian institution as Don Ho. In addition to hosting the Pro Bowl, the Hula Bowl, the Aloha Bowl, and eight NCAA games, the stadium is the venue for 130 high school games, including the Prep Bowl (a contest between the best private and public high school football teams). Aloha Stadium also features high school baseball, high school and semipro soccer, police department physical fitness programs, and that staple of all multiuse stadiums—monster truck events. It doesn't stop there. Aloha's biggest money-making event takes place outside the stadium in the parking lot. Three flea markets a week, year-round, yield $4 million in admissions and concession fees.

While maximum utilization of a stadium is an excellent means of bringing in the revenues to pay expenses and retire debt, there are risks involved in being a multiuse, multi-tenant facility. Just ask anyone who was at the Astrodome on October 10, 1980. An afternoon National League playoff game between the Astros and the Philadelphia Phillies went into extra innings and didn't end until 7:24 PM, six minutes before the scheduled 7:30 kickoff of a University of Houston-Texas A&M football game. Because the field had to be converted from baseball to football, the Houston-Aggies game didn't start until 11:33 PM. The contest ended with Houston beating Texas A&M 17-13 at 2:41 AM!

▶ Foxboro Stadium

The site for the construction of Foxboro Stadium was selected for its proximity to three of New England's largest cities—Boston, Massachusetts; Providence, Rhode Island; and Worcester, Massachusetts. ✐ *Official groundbreaking ceremonies for the stadium took place on September 23, 1970.*

In 1990 the United States was awarded the right to host the 1994 World Cup Soccer Championships. An initial list of the 35 prospective venues failed to include any New England site. Stadium management initiated an international lobbying effort to add Foxboro's name to the list. Joining forces with local tourism officials ultimately led to Foxboro's selection as one of nine host sites for the World Cup Games. Only Los Angeles and New York were awarded more than Foxboro's six games.

The World Cup has proven to be a harbinger of many successes in 1994. In addition to the World Cup, the stadium hosted eight national concert dates, the Drum Corps International Championships, and has been named the host site for Major League Soccer, the new professional soccer league, which will begin play in 1996.

Just 326 days later, on August 15, 1971, the Patriots christened their new home by hosting the New York Giants in an exhibition game. The home field helped give them a 20-14 advantage over the Giants before 60,423 fans.

Robert Kraft established an ownership position with the facility in 1989. In the fall of 1993 he became sole owner when he purchased his partner's interest in the stadium, a move that ultimately led to his ability to become the sole owner of the New England Patriots on January 21, 1994. Kraft's vision as owner has been to develop the facility into a nationally recognized family entertainment venue. By building and developing relationships with local officials and representatives of the music industry, Kraft and his associates have opened up the facility to more frequent samplings of diverse entertainment. In fact, Foxboro Stadium has hosted nearly three times as many special events in the past five years than it did during its first 20 years of operation.

National tours, of such groups as the Rolling Stones, The Who, and U2 have drawn record crowds to Foxboro. The stadium has worked to create unique events for the region, including the National Earth Day concerts and the Walden Woods concert in 1993.

Top left: Foxboro Stadium is home to the New England Patriots. Photo by David Silverman

Bottom left: Foxboro hosted six of the 1994 World Cup Soccer Championship games.

FOXBORO STADIUM QUICK FACTS

Constructed	September 23, 1970 - August 15, 1971
Playing Surface	Natural grass installed in 1991
Football Seating Capacity	50,794
Press Box Capacity	375 (122 seats for credentialed media)
Site Acreage	384 acres
Available Parking	16,000 automobiles

▶ The Louisiana Superdome

WELCOME TO THE TWENTY-FIRST CENTURY

The Louisiana Superdome is a monument to man's daring imagination, ingenuity, and intelligence. It has been dubbed a space-age wonder because of its awe-inspiring size and beauty, both of which are unique and unsurpassed. ➤ *It is more than merely another*

stadium. It is the most usable "people place" in the history of humankind. The Superdome's flexibility has enabled it to become a home to the nation's biggest sports and entertainment spectacles, while maintaining a schedule of day-to-day events.

The Superdome epitomizes football. Seating capacity for the Dome in its expanded football configuration is 76,791. The Dome has played host to the Nokia Sugar Bowl since the building's opening in 1975. Many of the games have held dramatic consequences as national championships rode on the outcome.

From the start, the Superdome has been the stage for some of the greatest Sugar Bowl games. On December 31, 1975, the game moved to the Superdome and Richard Todd led Alabama to a 13-6 win over Penn State in the first indoor Sugar Bowl. First-ranked Alabama (1980), Penn State (1983), and Miami (1990) all won national championships in the Dome, before crowds of 77,484, 78,124, and 77,452, respectively.

In 1990 Miami knocked off the SEC Champion Alabama, 33 to 25, to set the highest-scoring game in the Bowl's history. In winning the national championship, Miami's coach Dennis Erickson became only the second coach in college football history to do so in his first season at a school.

Numerous football greats have graced the Superdome's turf. Sugar Bowl players who performed in the Superdome and will not soon be forgotten include Tony Dorsett, Herschel Walker, Bo Jackson, Deion Sanders, and Steve Taylor.

The Nokia Sugar Bowl is not the only college game of national interest the Dome has to offer. The annual Bayou Classic between Grambling State University and Southern University has become a traditional game with national appeal. The Bayou Classic is the end-of-the-season rivalry played on Thanksgiving weekend before a sellout crowd of 76,000-plus.

The Superdome has provided more than a

showcase of the latest college talent. It has attracted events that have a huge economic impact on the city of New Orleans. The champion of all football games, the Super Bowl, has called the Louisiana Superdome home on five occasions. New Orleans has hosted more Super Bowls—seven—than any other city. (The first two were played at old Tulane Stadium.)

The Superdome's first Super Bowl, Super Bowl XII, January 15, 1978, set the trend for future games, as more than 86,000 visitors packed the French Quarter for a weekend of nonstop partying. In 1981 the Superdome donned a yellow ribbon in honor of the 52 American hostages who had just been released by Iran. That same year the Super Bowl brought more than $2.5 million to the city of New Orleans. In 1986 Ed McMahon declared on the "Tonight Show": "They ought to make New Orleans the Super Bowl City and

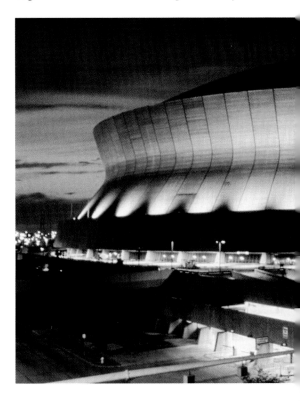

leave it right there."

Attendance records seem to be the Dome's forte. In 1981 the Rolling Stones brought the honor of the largest indoor concert crowd in history (87,500). The Superdome has also hosted the world's largest bingo party (12,000-plus) for the Lion's Eye and Ear Hospital Fund. It serves as the site for the Ringling Brothers, Barnum and Bailey Circus in the New Orleans area and for an annual Mardi Gras parade, the Endymion Extravaganza. The NCAA Final Four has held its Division I basketball championships in the Dome and brings world-record crowds: 64,959 were in attendance in 1987. The Superdome has hosted the SEC baseball tournament and is the annual site of the nation's premier regular season baseball tournament, the Winn-Dixie Showdown. The Dome will host the 1996 SEC Basketball tournament.

Construction began on the space-age beauty in 1971, and its doors opened on August 3, 1975. The magnitude of this 13-acre edifice is surpassed by no other domed stadium in the world. The Dome reaches 27 stories at its peak, forming the world's largest steel-constructed room unobstructed by posts. Seating capacity ranges from an intimate 14,000 to 87,500 for festival-style concerts.

The Superdome was the first large stadium to host a major political convention. Who can forget the exciting atmosphere at the 1988 Republican National Convention, with the Dome's 90-foot-high, sound-enhancing, royal blue drapery providing a regal background to the activities?

The Louisiana Superdome is managed by a private firm, Facility Management of Louisiana. Its parent company, Spectacor Management Group, operates more than 40 facilities worldwide. SMG is headquartered in Philadelphia and its facilities encompass 29 markets including the legendary Soldier Field in Chicago and the Los Angeles Coliseum.

The management agreement of the Superdome was a trendsetter in the industry. The Louisiana Superdome was the first publicly owned, privately run public assembly facility in the world. The Dome is owned by the Louisiana Stadium and Exposition District and leased by the State of Louisiana.

The Superdome is one of the top sightseeing attractions in the South, with an annual attendance of more than 75,000 tour patrons.

Although the Dome is home to the New Orleans Saints and the Tulane Green Wave, it is by no means just a sporting facility. It is a major office building, housing the New Orleans Sports Foundation (NOSF), a nonprofit, nonpolitical group; Nokia Sugar Bowl; Southwest Athletic Conference; ARAMARK Food Services; YMCA Fitness Center; the Greater New Orleans Tourist and Convention Commission (GNOTCC); and the Black Tourism Network. The latter two groups aggressively promote New Orleans as an important destination stop for tourists and conventioneers alike.

The Superdome is more than a stadium, building, or hall. It is the embodiment of Louisiana's belief in itself and a budding, exhilarating, moving certainty that tomorrow can be now.

The Superdome has been a great stage for football.

Left: The Louisiana Superdome's awe-inspiring beauty is unique and unsurpassed.

▶ Hubert H. Humphrey Metrodome

The NFL Super Bowl was held at the Metrodome in 1992.

Now in its 14th year of operation, the Hubert H. Humphrey Metrodome is a tribute to the civic leaders who championed building an indoor stadium in Minneapolis. Courtesy, Blakeway Publishing

The Metrodome's success story gives credence to the statement that it is unlike most other stadiums in the country—it was built on time, within its modest budget, and is entirely supported by user fees. No taxpayer monies have been spent for operations, maintenance, or bondholder

payments since year three of operation. Now in its 12th year of operation, the Hubert H. Humphrey Metrodome is a tribute to the civic leaders who championed building an indoor stadium in Minneapolis, Minnesota. It took courage and foresight. Today the only thing anyone argues about is which Metrodome event was the best.

Throughout the cavalcade of events that have danced in and out of the Metrodome's spotlight, three local teams have called the Metrodome home— the Minnesota Twins, the Minnesota Vikings, and the University of Minnesota Golden Gophers football team. All have set season attendance records. The Minnesota Timberwolves set an NBA single-season attendance record of 1,072,572 at the Metrodome in

their first year of play while awaiting completion of their permanent home. The Metrodome is the only stadium in the world to host the NFL Super Bowl (1992), Major League Baseball's All-Star Game (1985), two World Series (1987 and 1991), and the NCAA Final Four Men's Basketball Tournament (1992).

Not all of the Metrodome's colorful past involves the world of sports. Between the glitz and glamour of national sports championships, the Metrodome has continuously reinvented itself to accommodate a kaleidoscope of community events. Packed into its history are a parade of high school football championships, supercharged rock concerts, consumer shows, corporate events, and the solemn enormity of the National AIDS Quilt. Without missing a beat, the

Metrodome has been home to beach parties, volleyball leagues, police and firefighter training, major motorsport events, in-line skating, and two marriage ceremonies. A major motion picture, *Little Big League*, was filmed at the facility in 1993 and was released in mid-summer of 1994. Basketball aficionados immersed themselves in the NBA Jam Session during February 1994. The Rollerdome program saw a record 53,000 people enjoy in-line skating this past winter.

In October 1981 a blast from 20 electric 90-horsepower fans inflated the roof of the Metrodome, enabling the Minnesota Twins to play on the Super Turf for the first time in April 1982. The total cost for the facility was $80 million, including $55 million in base cost, investments by the Twins and Vikings for exclusive space, investment by the city of Minneapolis for reconfiguration of streets and utilities, donations by the business community for land, and other improvements. An additional 950 seats were installed early in 1994, including more seating between first and third base and expanded seating areas for disabled patrons. The year 1995 will bring a replacement of the artificial playing surface and a major expansion project totaling $20 million. Enhancements will include a plaza area at the new "front door" of the Metrodome, expanded women's restrooms and new family restrooms, widening of the upper and lower concourses, food courts, a new sound system, club seating and a lounge on the upper concourse, meeting room space, and various other amenities.

The phenomenal range of activities that have occurred under the 10-acre Teflon-coated fiberglass roof are a testimony to the memory of one of Minnesota's most revered statesmen, Hubert Horatio Humphrey. He is best remembered for his boundless optimism, for both the American people and good government. One of his last acts before succumbing to cancer in 1978 was to lobby for the construction of an indoor stadium in his home state. The success of a public facility such as the Metrodome is a living confirmation of Humphrey's faith.

▶ Kingdome

If it is possible for a public assembly facility to be "all things to all people," one need look no further than Seattle's Kingdome.  *This unique structure—it has the world's largest self-supporting concrete roof—is the home of the Seattle Seahawks of the National Football*

League and the Seattle Mariners of the American Baseball League. At one time it also housed the National Basketball Association Seattle SuperSonics and the Seattle Sounders of the North American Soccer League.

In addition to providing space and dates for Seattle's two Major League sports teams, the Kingdome functions as the Pacific Northwest's premier exhibit facility. With the recent addition of a 90,747-square-foot Pavilion, the Kingdome has become the largest display installation north of San Francisco.

The Kingdome is situated on a 48.4-acre site just south of Seattle's central business district. Constructed at a cost of $67 million, the building opened on March 27, 1976. The bond issue received 62 percent approval from King County voters after two previous attempts had failed. Recent roof renovations and ceiling repairs have created a bright appearance and have enhanced the stadium's image as an integral part of Seattle's skyline.

The Kingdome is a remarkable example of an all-purpose facility. Evangelist Billy Graham was an early visitor to the stadium and his 1976 eight-day Crusade attracted 434,100. The National Football League Pro Bowl recorded its first sell-out crowd on January 17, 1977, when 63,214 watched the AFC defeat the NFC, 24-14. The Kingdome had been open only two years when Major League

Baseball held its 50th All-Star Game there before a sell-out crowd of 58,905. World Cup exhibition soccer in 1976, 1979, and 1994, and the 1987 NBA All-Star Game, were hosted at the Kingdome as well.

The Kingdome was also the site of the 1984 NCAA Final Four basketball championships, which many college officials and coaches believe was the turning point at which it achieved recognition alongside the Super Bowl and the World Series. The Final Four has subsequently been held in the Kingdome—in 1989 and 1995. The stadium has also hosted four NCAA West Regionals, three of which set attendance records.

Some world-class entertainers have played before record attendance in the Kingdome. Paul McCartney and Wings, Linda Ronstadt and the Eagles, Aerosmith, The Who, and the Rolling Stones are a few of the groups to perform before large and enthusiastic crowds. The Stones attracted 137,160 fans in two nights at the Kingdome in 1981 and returned in 1994 to entertain 48,392 in a single performance.

The Kingdome's versatility has made the stadium a popular home for regional trade and consumer show promoters. The Seattle International Boat Show and International Sportsmen's Expo open the show season in early January. The Kingdome RV Show and the Seattle Home Show take place in February, while the Seattle International Auto Show plays in November, followed by the Christmas in Seattle gift show.

As testament to the building's multipurpose operation, the facility also hosts off-road racing and thrill shows. Amateur sports, such as Washington State high school championships, college baseball tournaments, and amateur football charity games round out the schedule.

Along with the Space Needle and Mt. Rainier, the Kingdome has become one of the region's best-known landmarks. During nearly 20 years of operation the Kingdome has been visited by more than 55 million people.

▶ The Montréal Olympic Stadium

Designed by French architect Roger Taillibert for the 1976 Games of the XXIst Olympiad, the Olympic Stadium is a unique architectural monument to one of the most memorable sports events in the annals of one of the world's great sports cities—Montréal! ▼ *An impressive concrete* structure, the stadium covers a mind-boggling 14.8 acres. It holds 56,000 seats and a playing field large enough to accommodate seven Boeing 747s or an enthusiastic crowd of Expos fans cheering on their team at an exciting Major League Baseball game. The Montréal Olympic Stadium has, in fact, been the home of the Montréal Expos since 1977.

Following the 1976 Summer Games, the stadium's adaptability was upgraded to accommodate a variety of professional sports activities, major entertainment events, and large-scale trade and consumer shows. Intended to ensure the stadium's profitability year-round, the revamping included the installation, in 1988, of a new floor with cabling for show exhibitors. Next, the seating design was modified to create a more intimate configuration better suited to the needs of professional sports.

The sound system was improved and, finally, in 1991-1992, new modern scoreboards were installed. That was also the year new retractable stands at the back of the baseball field linked the stadium to the Sports Centre and the Montréal Tower—the world's tallest inclined tower and a distinctive part of the city's skyline.

It's easy to see why Montréal Olympic Stadium has become one of Canada's leading, and busiest, venues for a wide range of national and international events. Not surprisingly, in 1990, it ranked as the American champion with 239 days of use.

But what kind of activities, specifically? Sports, for one! Major League Baseball, including the 1982 All-Star Game. Professional football, including four CFL Grey Cup games and the World Bowl in 1992. Soccer. SuperMo-

tocross racing. Stunt car shows. And the list goes on.

From the Pope to pop stars, the stadium has also been the stage of some of today's most unforgettable rallies and concerts.

In July 1977, Pink Floyd set attendance records. Emerson, Lake & Palmer, David Bowie, the Rolling Stones, Michael Jackson, Madonna—the greatest names in entertainment have performed here. In 1984 a youth rally for the visit of Pope John Paul II drew thousands to the stadium, and in June 1988, 60,000 opera buffs saw *Aïda* over two nights, setting a world record for opera attendance.

While the period from April to mid-October is given over to sports and concerts, during the remainder of the year the stadium is converted into Canada's largest exhibition hall under one roof. Every year the National Home Show, the Boat Show, the Recreational Vehicles Show, and the Auto Show attract thousands of fans while various trade fairs draw visitors and buyers from around the world.

The stadium features Canada's largest indoor parking facility—a total of 1.58 million square feet accommodating 3,600 cars as well as boarding docks for 50 buses. It is also accessible by subway.

Montréal's Olympic Stadium is an integral part of a series of installations known as the Olympic Park. These include a world-class swimming centre with six pools; Montréal Tower, with cable car whisking visitors to an observatory; and a Tourist Hall and the Biodôme (museum of the environment). It is also adjacent to Montréal's Botanical Garden and Insectarium.

In short, in addition to being one of North America's leading sports and entertainment facilities, Montréal Olympic Stadium is also a spectacular tourist attraction in its own right!

An interior shot of the stadium during an Expos baseball game (1993).

A rear view of the stadium.

▶ San Diego Jack Murphy Stadium

San Diego, California, is the home of one of America's finest multipurpose sports facilities. San Diego Jack Murphy Stadium was built in 1967 to accommodate a wide variety of events, ranging from baseball and football to concerts and off-road extravaganzas. *The stadium was*

renamed in 1981 to honor the late *San Diego Union* sports writer Jack Murphy, who initiated the metamorphosis of San Diego from a navy outpost to a world sports center by first convincing hotel magnate Barron Hilton to move his Chargers Football Team from their home at the Los Angeles Coliseum to San Diego. Murphy then led the charge to construct a world-class stadium in San Diego. The local architect selected to design the stadium, Frank L. Hope and Associates, had never designed a stadium before. Yet in 1969 San Diego Stadium became the only stadium to win the First Honor Award from the American Institute of Architects. The Hope firm also received a commendation award from Governor Ronald Reagan.

Expanded in 1983 to bring total permanent seating to 60,826, San Diego Jack Murphy Stadium has become the center of the San Diego sports scene. The city is the home of the San Diego Chargers of the NFL, the San Diego Padres of National League Baseball, and college football's San Diego State University Aztecs. The Holiday Bowl, one of college football's premier postseason bowl games, also takes place at the stadium each year.

Some of the outstanding sports events that have taken place at the stadium include the World Series in 1984, NFL Super Bowl XXII in 1988, and Major League Baseball's All-Star Games in 1978 and 1992.

Other popular events held regularly at the stadium include concerts, exhibition soccer, truck and tractor pulls, and supercross motorcycle races. In addition, the stadium parking lot accommodates such events as auto racing, swap meets, and car and RV sales.

In preparation for Super Bowl XXXII, which San Diego will be hosting in January 1998, the city is planning $50 million in improvements to the stadium. When completed, seating at the stadium will total 71,450, including 8,000 new club seats. The number of luxury skybox suites will be increased to 110. Other improvements include the construction of 20,000

square feet of office space, renovation of the Stadium Club, and the purchase of two new color boards. Concurrent with these improvements, the city has initiated an extension of the San Diego trolley that will include a stop on stadium property.

San Diego Jack Murphy Stadium has become the center of the city's sports scene.

▶ The ThunderDome

Opened in 1990, the ThunderDome is a 43,000-seat domed multiuse baseball stadium located in St. Petersburg, Florida. It was the first tension ring cable-supported domed baseball stadium to be built in the United States, and it is one of the largest in the world.

St. Petersburg's ThunderDome was the first tension ring cable-supported domed stadium to be built in the United States.

While designed for baseball, the ThunderDome hosts basketball, top-name concerts, hockey, football, ice shows, tennis, auto racing, equestrian events, motorcycle racing, consumer/trade shows, community festivals, and more. The Dome has the flexibility to accommodate from 10,000 to more than 50,000 people, depending on the event and configuration requirements.

The ThunderDome multipurpose features include:

- State-of-the-art movable grandstands that are set in various seating configurations to accommodate a wide spectrum of events.
- An 80-foot-high customized curtaining system that surrounds and creates the ThunderDome arena.
- A customized scrim system that can conceal the upper deck to provide additional intimacy for smaller arena events.
- A customized $1.5-million overhead concert rigging system that can hold more than 70,000 pounds of sound and light equipment.
- 2,200 amps of power adjacent to the stage area to drive concert sounds and lights.
- Custom-designed spotlight locations for six Xenon Bulb Gladiator Event Spotlights.
- 15 performer dressing room areas complete with dressing vanity, mirrors, lights, and furnishings.
- More than 6,000 on-site parking spaces.

The ThunderDome roof is an engineering marvel, resembling an open umbrella without the hands. Steel cables connected by struts support the roof, which is made of six acres of translucent Teflon-coated fiberglass. There are no fans needed to keep air pressure stabilized and no doors are pressure-locked. And the roof, which rises 225 feet above the floor area, allows natural light to shine inside the Dome.

With the arrival of Major League Baseball's Tampa Bay Devil Rays in 1998, additional features will be completed. These include a stadium club restaurant and lounge, a custom-designed and -built 9,000-square-foot home team clubhouse, customized team offices, luxury skybox suites, outfield scoreboard and video board, artificial turf, state-of-the-art in-house production facilities, and more.

Some sports and entertainment highlights include:

- The ThunderDome has been named as the site of the 1999 NCAA Men's Basketball Championship "Final Four."
- The ThunderDome, the City of St. Petersburg, and the University of South Florida hosted the 1994 first and second round sessions of the NCAA Men's Basketball Championships, setting new basketball attendance records for the state of Florida and the NCAA Southeast Region.
- The ThunderDome is the home of the NHL Tampa Bay Lightning until their new hockey arena is built. The Lightning holds the top 20 attendance records in the NHL, drawing more than 800,000 fans in the team's first year (1993-1994) in the Dome.
- The ThunderDome is home to the Arena Football Tampa Bay Storm. The Dome and the Storm hold all the Arena Football League attendance records, with the largest single-game record of 28,746.

Owned by the City of St. Petersburg and managed by the St. Petersburg Downtown Facilities Department, the ThunderDome is centrally located in the Tampa Bay area.

The ThunderDome can accommodate from 10,000 to more than 50,000 people, depending on the event and configuration requirements.

▶ Veterans Stadium

Soon after Shibe Park opened on April 12, 1909, people began calling

for the construction of a new stadium. The situation had escalated by

1953, the year that the park was renamed Connie Mack Stadium. The

building had become an eyesore. Parking around the old ballpark

had become congested, and the surrounding neighborhood had begun to deteriorate.

The movement for a new stadium suffered numerous setbacks, but a bond issue was passed by the voters and groundbreaking ceremonies were finally held on October 2, 1967. The total cost was projected at $40.5 million, with an additional $3.6 million for parking.

The first event held at the new Philadelphia Veterans Stadium was the 1971 baseball season opener between the National League Philadelphia Phillies and the Montreal Expos, with the home team winning 4-1. Attendance for the game was 55,352, the largest baseball gathering in Pennsylvania history at the time.

The first football game was played on August 16, 1971, a pre-season exhibition game between the NFL's Philadelphia Eagles and the Buffalo Bills.

Stadium appointments included a 126,000-square-foot AstroTurf® artificial playing surface and a state-of-the-art sound system. The high-tech scoreboard system was called "the largest, most expensive, and most sophisticated in all of sports." The scoreboards are gone now, replaced by a new giant-screen "Phanavision" and animated scoreboard.

In addition to being the favorite venue of the Army-Navy Football Classic, the "Vet" served as the home field for Temple University Owls football, a Big East Conference member, for more than 15 years. Notable rivals have included Penn State, Miami, West Virginia, and Syracuse.

Special events at the stadium have ranged from tractor pulls to professional wrestling and rock concerts, including performances by such headliners as the Rolling Stones, The Who, Bruce Springsteen, Madonna, U2, Paul McCartney and Wings, David Bowie, Pink Floyd, Wham,

Genesis, and the Beach Boys.

The City of Philadelphia Department of Recreation and the Phillies and Eagles have cooperated throughout the years to present a wide range of community-based events including local youth baseball, softball, and football tournaments, coaching clinics, charity auctions, and the like.

The regular infusion of capital dollars has ensured that the people of Philadelphia have a stadium in which they can take pride. Some $64 million has been invested in structural repairs, seat additions, and other improvements since 1985, and a $10-million program has been proposed for 1996 to complete the seating replacement on the lower levels, to improve outdoor lighting, to replace the AstroTurf® field, to extend the fire sprinkler system, to replace the remaining elevators, as well as to make various structural repairs and power plant upgrades.

Philadelphia's Veterans Stadium is home to the National League Phillies and the NFL's Eagles.

▶ Candlestick Park

Home to the San Francisco Giants National League baseball team and the San Francisco 49ers National League football team, Candlestick Park is the only stadium in the country to have hosted six NFC Championship Games. It has also been host to three Western Division Championships,

12 NFC West Conference Games, two World Series, and two All-Star games.

The history behind the naming of Candlestick Park is quite colorful. Candlestick Point and the cove in its embrace were named long ago after the indigenous candlestick bird. A member of the curlew family, the candlestick is a wading bird with long, thin legs and a body about the size of a chicken, according to nationally known ornithologist Henry L. Betten. At one time thousands of these birds inhabited the Bay Area, but they were nearly hunted to extinction by the 1950s due to the enormous demand for their delicate and delicious meat.

Ground was broken in 1958 and the first game at Candlestick Park was played on April 12, 1960, between the Giants and St. Louis. The then-near-capacity crowd of 42,269 watched the Giants beat the Cardinals 3-2.

In 1969 the stadium, which spans 14.5 acres on an 83-acre site, was expanded to seat 62,000 during football games and 59,000 during baseball games, becoming one of the first modern multipurpose stadiums. In order to keep its facilities and services up to date, Candlestick undergoes annual renovations each spring. The next renovation phase will increase seating capacity to 71,000. Phones for the hearing impaired have been installed, all restrooms are now wheelchair accessible, and the concourses were recently enlarged.

The stadium has six escalators, three passenger elevators, and one freight elevator. At one time its escalators were considered the longest in the country. There are four locker rooms, two first-aid stations, 2,000 locks, and 44 concession stands, including Perry Butler Catering. Parking capacity is an ample 8,000 cars, 300 buses, 200 limousines, and 300 motorhomes.

Brilliant lighting for night events is supplied by nine 140- to 240-foot towers, providing more than 350 foot-candles of light on the arena surface. It is considered to be the best-lighted stadium in the United States, literally turning night into day and exceeding the requirements of color television cameras. A new, state-of-the-art Sony video display board was installed in January 1994.

In addition to hosting baseball and football games, Candlestick Park holds ride and drive events in the parking lot, Mickey Thompson Off-Road Races, and rock concerts. In fact, the Beatles performed their last U.S. concert there on August 29, 1966. The Rolling Stones and Monsters of Rock concerts, in 1981 and 1987, respectively, each drew crowds of 85,000, and Pope John Paul II's 1987 visit attracted 86,000 people.

Candlestick Park captured the world's attention just before the start of Game 3 of the 1989 World Series between the San Francisco Giants and the Oakland A's, when a powerful earthquake struck Northern California. Despite the immediate loss of electrical power, stadium officials responded quickly to avoid a panicked response among the 65,000 spectators, and no one at the park was injured as a direct result of the quake. Possibly because the stadium had been undergoing "earthquake proofing" since 1983, there was no serious foundation damage. Cracked expansion joints and bleacher stairs were repaired by teams working around the clock and Candlestick Park was pronounced structurally sound. The game was rescheduled just 10 days after the catastrophe in what was considered to be a major stepping stone to the rebuilding of the Bay Area as well as a tremendous morale boost to beleagured local residents.

Owned by the city and county of San Francisco and operated by the Recreation and Park Department, Candlestick Park is home to baseball's Giants and football's 49ers.

▶ Commonwealth Stadium

Built to host the 1978 Commonwealth Games, Commonwealth Stadium

is conveniently situated less than one mile from downtown Edmonton,

Alberta. Seating over 60,000 people, with ample space for food conces-

sions, beverage sales, and souvenir stands, the stadium is the ideal venue

for sports, entertainment, and much more!

Home to the Edmonton Eskimos, the flagship franchise of the Canadian Football League, the stadium is no stranger to world-class events. In 1984 it played host to the Grey Cup, the CFL's Championship game. The stadium welcomed young athletes from around the world—in 1978 for the Commonwealth Games, and in 1983 to compete at the first North American held World University Games. In 1994 Commonwealth Stadium accommodated a sell-out crowd for a magical World Cup Soccer match between Brazil and Canada.

Commonwealth Stadium remains the only major sporting facility in Canada with natural turf, and is recognized as one of the premier playing surfaces in North America. This, combined with a three-story matrix scoreboard with instant replay and outstanding media facilities, makes the stadium an

ideal spot to showcase sporting events. Spectators are awestruck by the wide-open feel of the stadium, where you can expect the stunning backdrop of clear blue skies or the fiery northern lights.

Let's not forget entertainment! Over the years Commonwealth Stadium has become a major venue for concerts by such international stars as David Bowie, Willie Nelson, Genesis, Pink Floyd, and the Rolling Stones. Many of these performers have entertained sell-out crowds, including two Rolling Stones concerts that sold out in 49 minutes! In fact, Commonwealth Stadium was the top-grossing North American facility for the week of October 3, 1994, when the Stones played to 122,000 fans.

"The Jewel that is Commonwealth."

Football becomes a whole new ball game when played in a domed stadium. Pictured is a game of arena football. Courtesy, ThunderDome

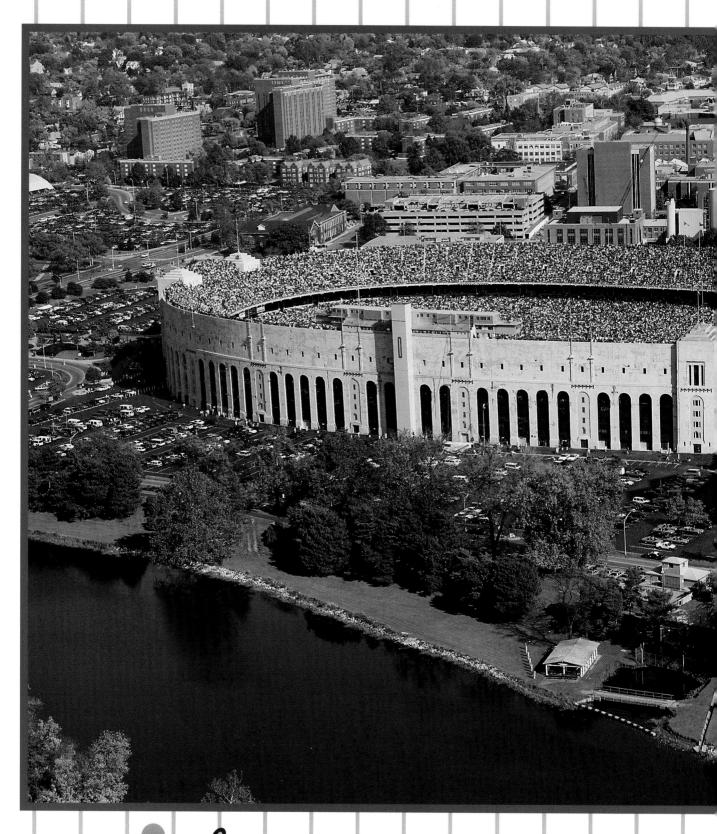

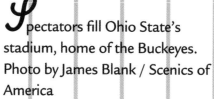

*S*pectators fill Ohio State's stadium, home of the Buckeyes. Photo by James Blank / Scenics of America

5

COLLEGE STADIUMS

Saturday's Heroes

Notwithstanding the recent spate of books, articles, films, and objects d'art glorifying baseball parks, college stadiums hold sway as America's most revered playing fields. Between Labor Day and Thanksgiving, no sports venue is more colorful, more festive, or more exalted than a college stadium on a football weekend. In the fall the stadium is the school and the school is the stadium, from the behemoths of the Big 10 and the Southeastern Conference to the more modestly proportioned Mid-America Conference and Ivy League.

At colleges and universities with strong athletic traditions, no structure on campus approaches the stadium in personifying the institution's image and heritage. For half a dozen splendid Saturdays a year, the stadium is the college's focal point, its center of gravity. Certainly few places on campus are as hallowed as the stadium. How hallowed? Says Mike Dolan, athletic facilities superintendent at Ohio State of the university's 73-year-old stadium, "The stadium is our cathedral."

The affection college stadiums enjoy has few equals in the annals of big-time spectator sports. What's different about college stadiums? What gives them their mythic quality?

What role do stadiums play in the changing environment of college athletics? And what does the future hold for college stadiums?

Whether they are megafacilities such as Michigan Stadium in Ann Arbor (capacity 102,000) or small stadiums such as Selby Field at Ohio Wesleyan (capacity 9,500), the appeal of college stadiums generally rests on three pillars: tradition, aesthetics and ambiance, and infrastructure.

Tradition. This is the mother's milk of college athletics. Many of the same sports fans who clamor for new major-league baseball parks and pro football stadiums would sooner see their own homes demolished than let the wrecker's ball touch their alma mater's gridiron. Age is not the issue for college stadi-

ums that it can be with professional facilities. In the opinion of many, the older a college stadium is, the better it gets. Some college stadiums even become world-famous tourist attractions. Reports Michigan Stadium supervisor Leon Tweedy, "People come from all around the world to see our stadium."

Of the five largest campus stadiums in the United States, Penn State's Beaver Stadium, built in 1960, is the newest. The remaining four—Michigan, Neyland (University of Tennessee), Ohio (Ohio State), and Stanford—date back to the 1920s, the heyday of college stadium construction.

Although constructed and dedicated in 1960, Beaver Stadium can trace its lineage to New Beaver Field, which was built in 1909 and used until 1959. Then it was dismantled, moved in 700 pieces to a campus site a mile away, and reassembled (with 16,000 additional seats) as Beaver Stadium.

The uniformity of architecture of many prominent college stadiums is also a tradition. According to Dennis Wellner, an architect with the HOK Sports Facilities Group:

College stadiums usually don't have the fit and finish of their professional counterparts. They are older, they seat more people, they're generally bowl or horseshoe-shaped, they have benched seating and, with the exception of accommodations for the press and guests of the institution's president, they often don't emphasize fan-friendly amenities the way pro facilities do.

The traditional design of so many well-known stadiums is not entirely coincidental. For example, consider that The Rose Bowl, built in 1922, was modeled after the Yale Bowl, which opened in November 1914 in response to the construction in 1903 of America's first concrete-and-steel stadium by rival Harvard. Princeton's Palmer Stadium, which bears a structural resemblance to Harvard Stadium, laid claim to being America's second-oldest football stadium by hosting its first game October 24, 1914, three weeks

before the opening of the Yale Bowl.

Meanwhile, in the Midwest, Notre Dame, bound for glory under coach Knute Rockne, wanted a stadium that would accommodate a growing following and chose the University of Michigan's stadium as a model. Rockne had a strong hand in the stadium's blueprint, communicating frequently with Osborn Engineering, the Cleveland firm that had designed not only Michigan's football stadium, but also Purdue's, Indiana's, and Minnesota's.

A hallmark of Rockne's design, a scaled-

A parachutist lands on the field of the Yale Bowl during the Yale-Harvard rivalry. Photo by Clark Broadbent

down version of Michigan Stadium, is the narrow space between the stands and playing field to keep "sideline guests" (as he called them) to a minimum. Rockne, who also supervised the new stadium's parking and traffic system, insisted that the new stadium be used only for football. Notre Dame Stadium opened in September 1930, four months after the beginning of construction, at a cost of $750,000.

While Knute Rockne lived to coach in his new stadium for only one year, Bob Neyland gradually built the University of Tennessee's stadium that now bears his name as he built the school's football program. Seating increased from 6,800 seats when he became

produced Super Bowl-winning quarterbacks Steve Young and Jim McMahon, flaunts its quarterback tradition in the Cougar Club Room of BYU Cougar Stadium. The Mid-America Conference's Miami University (Oxford, Ohio), which nurtured such coaching immortals as Paul Brown, Don Shula, Weeb Ewbank, and Red Blaik, has its "Cradle of Coaches" room in Yager Stadium.

Philanthropists, whose deep pockets and school spirit made possible so many playing fields, grandstands, press boxes, and weight rooms, are an integral part of the college stadium tradition. Their names, laid end to end, would run the length of a football field. Equally celebrated are coaches, statesmen, and educators. For example: Alabama's gridiron is named for coach Paul "Bear" Bryant; Duke's stadium is named for coach Wallace Wade; as previously stated, Neyland Stadium at the University of Tennessee bears the name of the coach credited with building the school's football program. Penn State's Beaver Stadium is named for James A. Beaver, a lawyer, Civil War general, superior court judge, Pennsylvania governor, and president of the university's board of trustees.

Stanford Stadium, the only college stadium to host a Super Bowl, is the permanent site of the Shrine East-West College All-Star football game and has hosted Olympic and World Cup soccer, as well as the U.S. Olympic

Left: Pasadena, California's Rose Bowl, built in the 1920s, is the current site of the UCLA Bruins' home games as well as other events. The stadium is modeled after the Yale Bowl, most probably because the president of the Tournament of Roses Association at the time of the stadium's construction grew up in New Haven, Connecticut. Photo by James Blank / Scenics of America

Neyland Stadium at the University of Tennessee seats about 100,000 spectators. Courtesy, University of Tennessee,

coach in 1926 to 52,000 when he retired in 1962. Neyland Stadium now seats more than 91,000 fans, a number that will increase to 101,000 in 1996.

Stadium tradition is bolstered by the memory of generations of athletic, philanthropic, and inspirational heroes.

Ohio Stadium boasts an Olympic running track upon which trots the ghost of Olympic immortal Jesse Owens. Outside the stadium are groves of trees, each tree planted when a Buckeye is named All-American. Virtually every major college stadium or athletic building features a hall-of-fame room for the benefit of misty-eyed alumni and starry-eyed recruits. Brigham Young University, which

The Rambling Wreck of Georgia Tech (Georgia Institute of Technology) host competing teams in this stadium located on the Atlanta campus. Photo by James Blank / Scenics of America

trials. In addition, the field on which quarterbacks Frankie Albert, Jim Plunkett, and John Elway strutted their stuff, remembers another, less athletic performer. In August 1928 Herbert Hoover, onetime student manager of Stanford's first football team, delivered a speech accepting the Republican presidential nomination in Stanford Stadium.

Aesthetics and ambiance. The scene is the season ticket holders' parking lot outside Cornell's Schoellkopf Field in Ithaca, New York, at noon on a football Saturday. While old grads and their guests munch and tipple their way through a variety of tailgate lunches, the Cornell marching band ambles up the hill from Barton Hall toward Schoellkopf Field, playing, as it has ever since the cars in the parking lot included Pierce-Arrows, George M. Cohan's "Give My Regards to Broadway." To decorous Ivy League applause, the band marches into the stadium, and the fans soon begin to follow. Inside Schoellkopf the view from the stands behind the Cornell bench and beyond the field's west

stands is of the West Hill mountain range, whose colors change magically as the sun moves westward. Whether Cornell wins or loses, fans can't help but leave this beautiful setting happy.

Wherever it takes place, a college football weekend is a theatrical occasion, and the stadium and its surroundings form the stage for its main event—Saturday's game. Many facilities were built with ambiance in mind.

In Seattle the University of Washington's Husky Stadium overlooks Lake Washington. On a clear day you can see Mount Rainier from the stands. Husky partisans claim it does not rain during football season. Neyland Stadium is close enough to the Tennessee River in Knoxville to encourage fans to get to the game by boat rather than car. The Ohio State University's stadium, on the Olentangy River in Columbus, boasts a rotunda studded with mosaics at its entrance. Over 35 years of expansions, Penn State has made a conscious effort to preserve Beaver Stadium's view of the Nitnanny Mountains. The University of

Virginia's Scott Stadium offers a view of Monticello, Thomas Jefferson's home. Columbia University's Lawrence A. Wien Stadium at Baker Field offers a panoramic view of the New Jersey Palisades as well as Spuyten Duyvil, the confluence of the Hudson and Harlem Rivers.

Kenan Memorial Stadium at Chapel Hill, North Carolina, seems to have been designed to make the most of its physical setting. The stadium is ringed by ancient pine trees that tower over the rim of the stadium. An even taller bell tower overlooks the pines. Tarheel folklore has it that when industrialist William Rand Kenan donated the land for the

Campus Stadiums: The Leaders of the Pack

STADIUM	CAPACITY
Michigan	102,501
Beaver (Penn State)	93,967
Neyland (Tennessee)	91,902
Ohio (Ohio State)	91,470
Stanford	85,500
Sanford (Georgia)	85,434
Jordan/Hare (Auburn)	85,214

stadium, he did so on the condition that the stadium would never rise higher than the pines. Writes one UNC alumnus, "As you approach the stadium, you feel like you're walking in the woods. All of a sudden, you're right next to a 48,000-seat football stadium." A 1927 editorial in the *Greensboro Daily News* said the designers of Kenan Stadium "have had a high sense of the fitness of things," adding, "It is completely surrounded by nature . . . it belongs to the hills and the woodland, and . . . they seem to belong to it."

Infrastructure. "We're constantly under a microscope here," says Mike Dolan of his responsibility for Ohio State's athletic facilities. Everybody—spectators, the press, alumni, potential recruits—expects everything to be perfect." The "everything" to which Dolan refers includes not only the playing field, but also stands, press boxes, parking lots, concessions, rest rooms, practice fields, and training, medical, and locker facilities. In addition, many stadiums are part of a school's athletic complex that may include facilities for other field sports such as soccer, lacrosse, or baseball and both natural and artificial surface football practice fields. While some major stadiums like those at Ohio State, Michigan, and Notre Dame are used for home football games only, others are open to all varsity field sports. Yale Bowl, for example, is the playing field for 33 Yalie teams, from men's lacrosse to women's field hockey.

For most stadiums, life is a constant cycle of renovations, modifications, and expansions. For example:

• The University of Maryland is completing a $30-$40 million renovation and addition to Byrd Stadium, which includes renovating the entire stadium building, restoring the seats, installing a five-story press box, and adding 14,000 seats, bringing the capacity up to 48,000.

• Notre Dame, pressed to provide alumni with more opportunities to see games, will have increased its seating capacity from 60,000 to 80,000 at a cost of $450 million in 1997. Other major improvements will include new rest rooms and concessions and a new press box.

• The University of Tennessee is increasing its stadium's seating capacity from 91,000 to more than 100,000 in time for the 1996 season.

• Tiny Ohio Wesleyan College (population 1,600) in Delaware, Ohio, has renovated 68-year-old football-only Selby Field to include an outdoor, all-weather track, a three-story press box with a president's box, and an enlarged playing field (with a new irrigation system) that accommodates lacrosse and field hockey as well as football.

Following page: This shot of a packed Brigham Young University Cougar Stadium offers a spectacular view of the mountains of Provo, Utah. Photo by Mark A. Philbrick / Brigham Young University

In 1995 the Southern Methodist University Mustangs selected the Cotton Bowl as their home field. The municipally owned and operated stadium is located in Dallas' Fair Park. Photo by James Blank / Scenics of America

While some colleges eschew the idea of luxury and premium seating as inimical to their spirit and tradition, others are taking pages from the NFL's playbook. The University of Georgia is adding 30 luxury suites, known as Sky Suites, to Sanford Stadium. The Sky Suites will seat 650 people. Using Joe Robbie Stadium in Miami as a model, the University of Florida is adding an end zone grandstand housing 18 suites, club seating, and 10,000 new seats. The University of Louisville is in the design stage of a new football stadium that will offer fan amenities comparable to those of an NFL facility.

Natural turf is making a comeback on major college gridirons. Three of the five largest on-campus stadiums—Neyland, Ohio, and Michigan—returned to grass since 1990. (Stanford and Beaver Stadium at Penn State had kept their natural surfaces throughout the Astroturf era.) Florida, Alabama, Mississippi, and South Carolina also made the switch from artificial to natural turf. In 1995 Virginia allocated a $5-million gift toward replacing the artificial turf in Scott Stadium with natural grass.

A major reason given for the reconversion to grass is that it is a powerful recruiting tool. Like state-of-the-art training facilities, a commodious locker room, and a pantheon of heroes in the hall of fame, a well-groomed grass playing field attracts the scholastic stars who are the life's blood of the Division IA schools. The University of Georgia adds a wrinkle of its own when its recruiters escort candidates and their parents along the pampered grass field of 85,000-seat Sanford Stadium—the players' names appear in lights on the electronic scoreboard.

While other spectator sports wax and wane, the juggernaut of high-quality college football rumbles eternally on. There are waiting lists forever for season tickets at the big football schools. Notre Dame alumni are relegated to a lottery system. Whatever the reason—one is that college teams don't move to cities with bigger television markets—college stadiums expect to keep packing the stands on those special Saturdays in the fall.

▶ Sun Devil Stadium

Originally erected between two mountain buttes in 1958, Arizona State

University's Sun Devil Stadium was literally carved from the desert, giving

it a spectacular setting in Tempe, Arizona, southeast of Phoenix. One of

the most dynamic, innovative, and beautiful stadiums in the nation,

this facility plays home to Arizona State football, the Fiesta Bowl, and the Arizona Cardinals, making it the only campus-owned stadium in the nation to host an NFL team.

Since its inception, Sun Devil Stadium has been expanded four times, resulting in a seating capacity of 74,200. Improvements in the past six years—costing over $21 million—have made the facility a football showcase.

The most recent major upgrade was a $1.67-million field renovation project that, when completed in June 1992, lowered and widened the playing surface. In addition to producing significantly more sideline space for players and the media, the improvement also eliminated sight-line problems that had caused obstructed views for patrons in the lower-row seats. Finally, 90,000 square feet of Tifway 419 sod was installed to cover the newly introduced field heating and drainage systems that were designed to promote growth during cooler months and quickly eliminate field water produced by heavy rains.

The bowl (south) end was connected in 1988 by Arizona State's dramatic Intercollegiate Athletic Complex (IAC), and an extension of the loge-level seats. This $8.9-million undertaking produced the exquisite 90,000-square-foot building that houses the entire realm of the ASU athletic department. A state-of-the-art video replay board and locker rooms in the north end were also added. The color video replay system, situated in the southwest corner, offers fans instant replays of game action, while a complimentary matrix board in the southeast corner provides messages and statistical information.

The press box and skybox facility, which sits atop the upper deck on the west side, contains two 30-suite levels and is topped by an ultra-modern press box and eight additional suites. This $11.9-million, 60,000-square-foot building offers working

space for more than 200 sportswriters, broadcast booths, booth space for statistical crews, coaches, public address personnel, security, scoreboard operations, and a rooftop camera deck in addition to suite seating for over 900 fans.

Besides staging 19 football games each year, Sun Devil Stadium has also presented a myriad of ancillary events. In 1987 the stadium—one of the few sites to host Pope John Paul II's tour of the United States—was filled beyond capacity for the papal visit. Further, this facility has staged numerous concerts and sporting events including, among others, the Rolling Stones, Paul McCartney, the Eagles, Mickey Thompson Off-Road Racing, and the World Cup Soccer Series. Of course, capping off this impressive list will be Super Bowl XXX in January 1996, one of the most recognizable events to be held worldwide.

Clearly, the magnificent setting, coupled with the striking additions, have made Sun Devil Stadium one of the true showcases of not only college and professional football, but of outdoor entertainment as well.

Sun Devil Stadium is home to Arizona State football, the Fiesta Bowl, and the Arizona Cardinals.

▶ Legion Field Stadium

One of the most recognizable stadium names in the country, Legion Field has been synonymous over the years with Alabama football at all levels, including the University of Alabama, Auburn University, the University of Alabama-Birmingham (UAB), the Magic City Classic, and small colleges

and high schools. Hundreds of games have been and continue to be played in this historic edifice.

There's an old saying that if you have a good piano, you will attract good piano players. The same is true in football stadiums. Legion Field is historically one of the top 10 in the country.

Great stadium, great coaches, great players. Run down a partial list of the superior coaches whose teams have played here—Wallace Wade, General Bob Neyland, Frank Thomas, Bobby Dodd, John Vaught, Wally Butts, John McKay, Tom Osborne, Gene Stallings, and Pat Dye, to name a few. Add to those, from the pro ranks, Tom Landry, Joe Gibbs, Hank Stram, Paul Brown, Curly Lambeau, and Jack Pardee and you begin to get a feel for the history of this site.

The most notable coaches, however, would have to be Paul "Bear" Bryant and Ralph "Shug" Jordan, who for years shared their Alabama and Auburn rivalry here. In fact, the game is still contested at Legion Field on a regular basis, and still creates the same fire and fury as before.

Great players. Too numerous to name, but think of Don Hutson, Harry Gilmer, Pat Sullivan, Terry Beasley, Joe Namath, John Stallworth, and Bo Jackson. The list could go on and on.

Legion Field is a municipal stadium operated by the City of Birmingham, through its Park and Recreation Board and their stadium manager. The average annual program for Legion Field consists of 15-20 college and professional football games, concerts, and other special events.

Begun in 1926, the stadium was opened to its inaugural game featuring Howard College (now Samford University) vs. Birmingham-Southern College, on November 19, 1927. The first major college game was Alabama vs. Georgia on November 27, 1927.

The stadium was named Legion Field in 1927, in honor of the American Legion, and stands as a memorial to those who gave their lives in the service of their country.

As with all municipal stadia, Legion Field has experienced growth by degrees. Some five or six different expansion efforts have been undertaken over the years.

Historically, Legion Field has been involved with several professional leagues (the latest being the Canadian Football League beginning in 1995); and with college bowl and playoff games, including the first—and only—World Bowl, held in 1974; the annual Hall of Fame Bowl for 10 years; and ultimately the first two history-making SEC Championship games, held in 1992 and 1993.

Birmingham's Legion Field Stadium has been synonymous over the years with Alabama football at all levels.

▶ Rose Bowl

The nation's most famous college football stadium—the Rose Bowl—located in Pasadena, California, currently seats 100,086. The stadium was built in two phases: the north horseshoe in 1922 and the south

end in 1928. One of the finest stadiums in America, the Rose Bowl was built specifically for football, but was used for portions of the 1932 Olympic Games and was also the soccer site for the 1984 Olympics. The Rose Bowl has also been the site of five Super Bowls, and was recently the championship venue for the 1994 Soccer World Cup. Known as "The Granddaddy of Them All," the stadium annually hosts the Rose Bowl Game—played around New Year's—featuring champion teams from the Big 10 and Pacific Coast conferences. The stadium is now in its second decade as the home of the UCLA Bruins. It is also the site of the world-famous R.G. Canning Flea Market, held the second Sunday of each month.

The Rose Bowl is America's most famous college football stadium.

▶ Cotton Bowl Stadium

Owned and operated by the City of Dallas, the Cotton Bowl has a capacity of 72,000 with the inclusion of portable bleachers. The stadium is located in the heart of Fair Park, a 277-acre complex designated a national

The Cotton Bowl is located in the heart of Dallas' Fair Park.

historic landmark that is noteworthy for having the largest existing collection of Art Deco-style exposition buildings in the United States. Just two miles from downtown Dallas, Fair Park has the highest concentration of cultural facilities in Dallas as well as 749,000 square feet of leasable space. The leasable buildings have worked superbly for staging events in conjunction with stadium games and concerts, thereby providing promoters with a unique source of additional income.

In 1992 and 1993, $14 million in improvements/renovations to the Cotton Bowl were completed. These included the installation of a Class A grass field with subdrainage and irrigation systems, refurbishment of the existing press boxes, and the replacement of the mechanical, electrical, and plumbing systems on the west side of the stadium.

The Cotton Bowl, which accommodates 67,600 spectators for international soccer, was one of the nine United States venues for six World Cup 1994 games. The stadium has been the home field for professional soccer and football teams, including the Dallas Cowboys.

Annual events in the stadium include the New Year's Day Mobil Cotton Bowl Classic, Texas versus Oklahoma University, and the Al Lipscomb Classic featuring Grambling University and Prairie View A&M. In 1995 the stadium was again selected by Southern Methodist University as the site for its home games through the year 2000.

𝒮an Francisco's Candlestick Park has been selected as the site of Super Bowl XXXIII in 1999. According to the NFL's Director of Special Events, Super Bowl preparations cost $750,000 to $1.2 million (all paid for by the NFL). Courtesy, Candlestick Park

6

STADIUM OPERATIONS

Getting Ready for the Next Event

Put yourself in Jim Duggan's chair during the final week of August 1994. The manager of Chicago's 67,000-seat Soldier Field, Duggan was looking at a schedule of events formidable enough to send a Washington hostess into a tizzy:

Saturday, August 27, 7:00 PM,
Chicago Bears vs. New York Giants

■

Thursday, September 1, 7:00 PM,
University of Illinois vs. University of Washington

■

Saturday, September 3, 7:00 PM,
Notre Dame vs. Northwestern

■

Sunday, September 4, 12:00 noon,
Chicago Bears vs. Tampa Bay Buccaneers

By the time the final gun of the Bears-Bucs game signaled the end of the week of August 27, Soldier Field's grass playing surface had been mercilessly pummeled by roughly 30 tons of football players, while its seats, concourses, rest rooms, and concession stands had withstood the collective enthusiasm of some 270,000 spectators.

The following Sunday and Monday nights (September 11 and 12), the venerable 70-year-old Greco-Roman sports palace weathered an onslaught by an estimated 200,000 rock fans thronging to two 7:30 PM to midnight performances of the Rolling Stones.

The morning after the last Stones devotee departed the stadium, Duggan's ground crew stripped Soldier Field of its ravaged turf and replaced it 24 hours later with a 2,400-square-yard carpet of fresh two-inch-thick sod pieced together like a gigantic jigsaw puzzle. By the time the "Monsters of the Midway" rumbled onto the field less than 72 hours after the laying of the new sod, the groundskeepers had provided them with a brand-new playing surface, complete with bright new yard, end zone, and sideline markers.

At the same time the field was being refurbished, 100 workers toiled through the night, cleaning the stadium's 67,000 seats, concourses, and ramps. At least as many more laborers scoured the stadium's 38 rest rooms, while others changed light bulbs and fixed broken seats. A contract cleaning service scrubbed 116 luxury boxes and the press area. Three garbage trucks arrived at midnight to haul away the debris of the previous evening's festivities.

Says Duggan, "At a stadium, you never stop getting ready for the next event." He could have added that every time a stadium opens its gates, a structure that traditionally occupies only a few square blocks or the space of a rural pasture becomes the equivalent of a major metropolitan center. For example: A sellout crowd of 45,000 at Oriole Park at Camden Yards in Baltimore equates to the population of Fort Myers, Florida. With 80,000 seats, the Pontiac Silverdome, outside Detroit, can accommodate every man, woman, and child in Sioux City, Iowa. Filled to its 70,000-plus capacity, the University of Nebraska's Memorial Stadium is the Cornhusker State's third-largest city. The Rose Bowl can seat every one of Erie, Pennsylvania's 110,000 inhabitants. And any major stadium that is the venue for a rock concert, religious revival, or political rally can host upwards of 160,000 people (the combined populations of Danbury, Connecticut, Daytona Beach, Florida, and Galveston, Texas).

Like a modern city, a stadium is a round-the-clock operation supported by an infrastructure of power, sanitation, communications, maintenance, and security that provides paying customers with such benefits as ample parking; clean, well-lighted facilities; police protection; convenient concessions; and access and seating for the disabled.

Also like a city, a stadium has to meet a payroll, provide emergency medical care, and carry insurance against calamities ranging from business interruptions caused by fire, vandalism, inclement weather, and natural disasters to outlandish personal injury liability claims. It must also honor contractual arrangements with suppliers of everything from state-of-the-art electronic score boards to such basic services as masonry, electrical, plumbing, heating, ventilating, and air-conditioning services. The Convention, Sports and Entertainment Consulting unit of KPMG Peat Marwick puts the average annual budget for these operations—exclusive of maintaining the playing field—at more than $3 million.

The more events put on in a stadium, the more its managers and staffs have to do to make sure these events come off successfully. "Like any business, a stadium depends on repeat business," says Bill Squires, manager of Giants Stadium, in East Rutherford, New Jersey. "We want to keep the facility safe, clean and inviting so that fans will come back and

Facing page: Chicago's Soldier Field has a seating capacity of 67,000 for football games. Photo by James Blank / Scenics of America

promoters will keep booking events with us."

Every stadium consists of two basic components: the playing field and the stands. It takes an awful lot of work to keep both running properly.

THE FIELD: SETTING THE TONE FOR THE STADIUM

The field, whether artificial or natural turf, sets the tone for the stadium. Texas Rangers groundskeeper Jim Anglea, who tends the turf at The Ballpark at Arlington and who put a less-than-optimum Cleveland Stadium playing field into respectable shape in the 1980s, puts it this way: "The first thing a fan does when he walks through the gate is look at the field."

Groundskeepers make sure that the first sight of the field is a favorable one. They also keep the field between the foul lines and sidelines resilient and as free as possible of the ruts and snags that can injure an athlete. A stadium's alchemists, groundskeepers blend soils, sands, grasses, fertilizers, and pesticides to provide a perennially green carpet and smooth base paths of a uniform consistency and hue. They design and install irrigation and drainage systems that prevent puddles from forming on playing surfaces and repair the perennial scuffs around home plate and on pitchers' mounds. They deploy protective tarps weighing as much as 3,000 pounds to protect a field against rain and snow. And they even go so far as to replace every divot torn up during a ball game or a concert.

Groundskeeping, like "women's work," is never really done. Writing in *Athletic Business* magazine, Tom Lujan, field manager of Mile High Stadium in Denver, comments:

Proper game preparation will take almost a week. You'll spend Monday through Wednesday watering and cutting the field and part of Thursday painting. It takes eight to 12 hours to paint logos on the field. After the game, secure all equipment and water the field. Walk the field the next morning, pushing any divots back, hand-raking it if you can. Remove clippings and excess grass kicked up by cleats.

The Rangers' Jim Anglea, who once boasted of being at his stadium every day of the year but Christmas, described the groundskeeping process in a more personal way to a meeting of minor-league baseball executives in 1983, shortly after he joined the Cleveland Indians:

I cut the infield twice a day, both ways. I will cut my outfield twice, both ways. I do this by myself. I will fix the mound, I'll fix home plate, I'll fix the bullpens . . . A good groundskeeper will [always] come in and check in with his job. He just won't stay away.

The greatest challenges stadiums face today are preserving the field in the face of a mounting schedule of events and having the flexibility to meet unusual demands. Many multiuse, multievent stadiums opt for durable, impact-resistant artificial turf to withstand the rigors of rock concerts, motorcycle races, and tractor pulls. Natural turf venues are finding other solutions such as turf-protection covers made of heavy-gauge polyester and perforated to let air and sunlight get to the grass and soil. These same covers are used increasingly to protect the infield against scuffs during pregame batting practice. Turf-protection covers also form a

Workers lay sod for the field of The Ballpark at Arlington in early 1994, prior to the stadium's opening. Courtesy, Texas Rangers

layer between the turf and sheets of plywood covered by tons of dirt for vehicular events.

THE STANDS: THREE DAYS TO RECOVER, TWO DAYS TO PREPARE

A stadium's building and occupants need as much tender, loving care as its playing field. The seats, concourses, rest rooms, lights, elevators, escalators, and other facilities and services have to be cleaned, maintained, and repaired. Ushers, security forces, maintenance people, and cleanup crews have to be scheduled. Safety and order have to be maintained. Concession stands have to be stocked. Paying customers have to be parked, guided, seated, protected, disciplined, fed, and cleaned up after.

No detail is overlooked. The general manager of one minor-league team told a conference of his peers that he and his cleanup crews go on "gum patrol" after every game. "The crew goes through the entire ballpark looking for gum," he said. Everybody carries a putty knife to scrape gum off the seats and the stands."

Says manager Bill Squires, whose busy Giants Stadium is the venue for 30 NFL and college football games a year, "We have three days to recover from one event and two days to prepare for the next one."

San Diego Jack Murphy Stadium, at 125 events a year, is the busiest grass-surface stadium in the United States and a textbook example of how fast a stadium has to run to stay fresh for its patrons. Home to baseball's Padres, the NFL Chargers, and the San Diego State football team, Jack Murphy also attracts more than its share of events such as national religious revivals, crafts shows, and tractor pulls. Even when the stadium itself is dark, Jack Murphy is busy. Led by recreational vehicle shows, car sales, and auto races, Jack Murphy's parking lot is the scene of a revenue-producing event every day of the year.

The stadium's sports calendar is especially crowded in the early fall, when baseball and football overlap, and the crews undertake the 10-hour process of reconfiguring

baseball seating to football seating, only to return it to baseball (all within fewer than three days). Maintenance and cleaning at Jack Murphy are continuous. Is there any difference between baseball and football when it comes to after-game maintenance? Assistant stadium manager Stephen Shushan describes post-football maintenance as "more intense" than baseball. "We get more broken seats after a football game," he says.

Among the time-honored treats associated with baseball games are hot dogs, peanuts, and cotton candy. Here a vendor at Oriole Park at Camden Yards sells one of these tasty refreshments to hungry fans. Courtesy, ARAMARK Corp.

Customer service is becoming a standard part of operations at Jack Murphy Stadium and other facilities. For example, Jack Murphy has a customer service department to hear and act on customer complaints. In Toronto all 750 full- and part-time SkyDome employees attend Sky-Dome University, a training program modeled after those at Disney World and McDonald's Hamburger U., that emphasizes customer awareness and satisfaction. Under SkyDome University posters urging them to be "aggressively friendly," employees from executives to cleaners are introduced to subjects from "measuring customer satisfaction" to "techniques to deal with impaired guests." Asked by the *Toronto Star* why he puts as high a value as he does on SkyDome U., Sky-Dome president Richard Peddie said, "We believe in continuous improvement. We didn't want to be just a jock-and-rock place."

Security is taking on greater importance among stadium operations. "People come to enjoy themselves," says Rich Ryan, who heads security for Giants Stadium. "It's our job to make sure they do just that." With a full-time security staff of 200, Ryan stays alert for eventualities ranging from terrorism to lost children to unruly fans. He also employs roving details in the parking lot and on access roads scouting for ticket scalpers and unauthorized vendors.

"Our people watch the stands with binoculars, and we have six video cameras that scan the stadium and parking lot and can zoom in on one seat if necessary," says Ryan. "In one case, we zoomed in on an unauthorized balloon vendor in the parking lot and found that he was selling balloons filled with nitrous oxide to customers who wanted to get a cheap high."

Two postscripts about stadium security. First, the large concentration of people at a sellout event make terrorism a constant threat. In January 1991, for example, in the midst of the Gulf War, Tampa Stadium's security force put every one of the more than 75,000 spectators attending the Super Bowl through metal detectors after threats of a terrorist attack. Second, a little known fact about the scope of stadium security operations is that most large stadiums have holding cells. Yankee Stadium even has its own NYPD precinct.

If, as Texas Rangers groundskeeper Jim Anglea says, the first thing you see when you enter a stadium is the field, the second sighting is almost certain to be a concession stand. That's understandable because food and beverage service is probably the largest and most visible operation in a stadium. It can also be the most complex. Just ask Paul Picardi, who provides food and drink for upwards of 75,000 hungry and thirsty fans a week at Giants Stadium as a regional representative of sports catering leader Harry M. Stevens, Inc. "We begin preparing for a game three days ahead and don't stop taking deliveries until two hours before the game," says Picardi, who oversees 700 employees operating 40 concession stands, 10 vending stations, and 100 portable refreshment stands.

The centerpiece of the operation is an 8,000-square-foot central commissary, including a spacious refrigeration area, that is fed from loading docks on the ground level. Supplies are distributed from the commissary to the concession stands, each of which has its own walk-in refrigerator. What sells the most, says Picardi, depends on the time of year. "The weather is the biggest determinant in our sales picture," Picardi says. He continues:

During the hot weather, we push out as much cold beverage as we can. We operate a 30-foot-high silo that makes ice all week long before an event. Then as the weather cools, food takes off. On a 40-degree day during football season, we sell 25-30,000 hot dogs and 20,000 soft pretzels, which are popular in the New York metropolitan area. When the weather really gets cold, hot liquids take over. We sell 800 gallons of coffee and 1,200 gallons of hot chocolate at December and January events.

Concession operations also respond to the tempo of a particular event. "Baseball crowds and football crowds have different buying patterns," says Picardi, who once ran Harry M. Stevens' operations in Fenway Park, home of the Boston Red Sox. As Picardi states:

Baseball has 18 mini-intermissions in a nine-inning game, and people usually come to concession stands when their team isn't at bat. Football is a high-intensity game with strict intermissions. We have two business windows—one about half an hour before kickoff, the other at half-time.

Like a stadium's other operations, concessionaires follow the cleanup-preparation cycle. "It takes us two days following a game to clean up and three days to replenish for a Sunday game," says Picardi. "We don't stop delivering until two hours before game time, when we distribute fresh hot dog and hamburger rolls."

Then, like the groundskeepers, cleanup crews, tradesmen, and everyone else involved in a stadium's operations, Picardi spends his time getting ready for the next event.

Getting Ready for Super Sunday

Congratulations, Candlestick Park. You're going to be the site of Super Bowl XXXIII in 1999. You'd better start planning for it now because you've got a lot of work to do.

"No stadium in the world can handle a Super Bowl without special preparation," say Jim Steeg, the NFL's Director of Special Events and the man who has been in charge of Super Bowl preparations since 1980. Says Steeg:

While the extent of the modifications depend on the stadium, the league requires an increase in seating and parking, upgrades of lighting and sound systems, and the installation of a jumbo video board. We triple security and accommodate at least six times the number of media that usually cover an NFL game. And that's only the beginning.

Steeg adds that Super Bowl preparations cost $750,000 to $1.2 million, paid for by the NFL.

Architect Jerry Anderson, Managing Director of Anderson DeBartolo Pan of Denver, is in charge of implementing the prerequisites laid down by Steeg and the NFL. "Preparing a stadium for a Super Bowl is a major piece of temporary work," says Anderson. "For example, we have to build 600 tabletops for media and add 500 press seats with clipboards as the number of press people increased from a normal complement of 150 to 750."

Also in the area of media coverage: temporary booths for 16 foreign voice origination and 50-60 satellite units outside the stadium. Steeg recalls almost wistfully that when he began working the Super Bowl in 1980, most reporters used typewriters. "Then technology took over, and we had to add wiring for computers, modems, and faxes," he says.

"There are so many events in a Super Bowl, we have to cycle them," says Anderson. For example:

The stage for half-time entertainment during the game becomes an interview room for 400 reporters after the game. And because it isn't Super Bowl day without a celebration, the stadium has to prepare to accommodate an increased number of tailgate parties. To accommodate the heavy corporate patronage that Super Bowls generate, a 300,000- to 400,000-square-foot corporate hospitality village goes up outside the stadium.

What if stadiums were built to meet all the Super Bowl's requirements? "Not practical," says Anderson. "The game keeps getting bigger, and a stadium built to Super Bowl scale in, say, 1996, would have to be upgraded for 1997."

The media prepare for Super Bowl XXIX at Joe Robbie Stadium in Miami.

PHOTO BY AL MESSERSCHMIDT. COURTESY, ANDERSON DEBARTOLO PAN

▶ ARAMARK

Think back to your first trip to a professional baseball or football game.

The clamor of the crowd, the cheering and the jeering. The thrill of a

ninth-inning home run. Or a long touchdown pass in the closing seconds

of the game. ☛ *Think back and you'll surely remember, too, the*

indescribable pleasure of biting into a steaming hot dog, slathered in mustard and nested in a bun lined with nuggets of crunchy relish.

For us at ARAMARK, serving up memorable hot dogs to sports fans—or pizza, sausage and ribs, for that matter—involves as much professional expertise as a successful extra-base hit or end-run.

You see, every year our Leisure Services Group provides catering, concession, recreation, lodging, and retail services to more than 50 million people at stadiums, arenas, parks, resorts, and racetracks all across America. And that's only a part of what we do.

Our business is managed services—for businesses, hospitals, schools, and colleges. The fact is, we're the leader in the field. Like any winning team, we've compiled a host of impressive stats. Here's one example, to give you an idea of the kind of numbers we're talking about: Each year we serve over 400 million meals.

As you might expect, operating on such a scale requires consummate professionalism at every level.

We've achieved that by creating an environment where every job is recognized as requiring its own special expertise. Proficiency and performance are what count. Individual initiative is encouraged. Which is not much different, really, from team sports. It's a great thing to have a lineman intercept a pass when the ball comes flying his way.

In the nearly 30 years we've been in sports, our commitment to professionalism has won us a place on the stadium roster of some of the best-known teams in the country.

In Major League Baseball, we're with the Atlanta Braves, Baltimore Orioles, Boston Red Sox, Colorado Rockies, Houston Astros, Los Angeles Dodgers, Montreal Expos, New York Mets, and Pittsburgh Pirates.

In the National Football League, we're at home with the Denver Broncos, New York Giants, New York Jets, New Orleans Saints, Chicago Bears, and Pittsburgh Steelers.

We're in the National Basketball Association and the National Hockey League, too. We're at courtside with the Cleveland Cavaliers, Houston Rockets, Miami Heat, New Jersey Nets, and San Antonio Spurs. We're at rinkside with the Florida Panthers, New Jersey Devils, New York Islanders, Pittsburgh Penguins, and San Jose Sharks. When the Philadelphia 76ers (NBA) and the Flyers (NHL) move into Philly's new CoreStates Spectrum II arena, now under construction, we'll be moving with them.

Through our many team associations, we've been privileged to share in landmark events. Willie Stargell winning the MVP award and the Pirates winning the World Series in 1979, for example. Andres Galarraga, of the Colorado Rockies,

Coors Field in Denver continues the tradition of giving the fans the feel of an old-time ballpark with all the modern amenities at convenient locations.

slugging his way to the National League batting championship in 1993. The 1994 concert by tenors Luciano Pavarotti, Placido Domingo, and José Carreras that played to a packed house at Dodger Stadium—and to a global television audience estimated at over one billion people.

And we're not just serving hot dogs anymore. An important factor in our success has been staying close to customers—learning their food preferences and, where appropriate, adapting our menus to suit regional tastes.

At Oriole Park, for example, it's Maryland crabcakes and former Oriole great Boog Powell's barbecue.

At Three Rivers Stadium it's nachos and the Primanti's sandwich—meat, cheese, cole slaw, tomatoes, and french fries—all of it layered between two hearty slices of fresh-baked Italian bread.

At the Superdome, it's jambalaya, a mix of rice, sausage, and chicken.

At Coors Field, it's buffalo sausages and burgers.

We've even regionalized the humble hot dog, itself, with the Dodger dog at Dodger Stadium (what else?).

Responding to change has been vitally important to our growth. We constantly monitor food trends, not just by reviewing statistical data but by listening to our customers, the facility operators, and to their customers—the public "out there" in the stands. So you'll notice that our menus now include specialty items such as bottled water, wine selections, frozen

yogurt, salads, and even special kids' meals.

Giving people what they want: That's the name of the game for us at ARAMARK. It's made our team of professionals the leading players in managed services for food, refreshments, uniforms, child care, medical services, facilities management, and magazine and book distribution.

ARAMARK has provided food, beverage, and retail merchandise services at Atlanta Fulton County Stadium for nearly 30 years.

Pregame business booms on Eutaw Street, adjacent to Oriole Park at Camden Yards in Baltimore. ARAMARK's managed services are a key to the ballpark's success.

► Southwest Recreational Industries, Inc.

ASTROTURF® . . . THE SURFACE OF CHAMPIONS

The Cowboys, Bills, Steelers, Falcons, Vikings, Oilers, Bluejays, Pirates, Astros, Cardinals, Longhorns, Spartans, and thousands of other well-known sports organizations in the high school, college, and professional ranks all have at least two things in common: They are champions and

Home of the Atlanta Falcons and Super Bowl XXVIII, the Georgia Dome floor has more than 102,000 square feet of AstroTurf® and hosts nearly 300 events each year, generating $209 million in annual revenue, $13 million in new taxes, and an estimated 1,900 new jobs in Georgia since opening in 1992.

they play on AstroTurf® in multipurpose stadiums that serve their communities hundreds of times each year.

practice and compete at home on AstroTurf®.

ASTROTURF® IS NOT A TREND. . .IT IS A FOUNDATION OF SPORTS

More amateur and professional events, like the World Series, Super Bowl, Sugar Bowl, Sun Bowl, Hula Bowl, Peach Bowl, and many major conference championships, are now played on Astro-Turf® in North America than on any other sports surface. Today more than half of the NFL and Major League Baseball franchises and NCAA football teams

RISING THROUGH THE MUD AND SNOW TO PROVIDE SOLUTIONS

In more than 30 years synthetic turf has grown from a research curiosity to a major component of sports programs and multiuse stadiums. During the 1950s the Ford Foundation initiated studies to improve the physical fitness of young people, particularly for city kids whose options were often limited to paved, fenced, or dangerous surfaces. In conjunction with Monsanto's efforts in the early 1960s, the first large-scale experimental installation was made at the Moses Brown School in Providence, Rhode Island, in 1964. This original surface provided more than 25 years of service under very heavy usage.

In 1965 Judge Roy Hofheinz finished construction of what he billed as one of the world's wonders in Houston, Texas—the "AstroDome." Faced with reduced sunlight and heavy usage, a new synthetic surface was developed and installed by opening day in 1966 for the Houston Astros and later that year the

Dyche Stadium, constructed in 1926, is one of AstroTurf®'s newest members, installing a new state-of-the-art field in 1994. The stadium hosts home games for the Big Ten Conference Wildcats team and many other events throughout the year.

football field was ready in time for the Houston Oilers' season.

The world's first multipurpose, multisport facility now had more than 125,000 square feet of "AstroTurf®." Many stadiums followed the AstroDome's lead and installed AstroTurf for amateur and professional events over the next 25 years.

ASTROTURF® HAS MET THE TEST OF TIME

Since the early days in Houston, many others have tried to imitate AstroTurf® but have not survived. Only AstroTurf® has constantly remained in use over three decades, continues to make improvements, and has grown substantially in use throughout North America, Europe, and the Far East.

MEETING THE DEMANDS OF ALL AMERICANS

The commitment by AstroTurf® to providing safe and high-quality sports surfaces has allowed millions of Americans numerous opportunities for sports and recreation throughout the year, every year, regardless of weather or schedules.

As major partners in this commitment, stadium owners and managers have long recognized the increased pressure to provide year-round facilities and surfaces that can meet both usage demands and financial pressures faced by their facilities. Today many stadiums with AstroTurf® host more than 200 events each year, helping to develop the next generation of athletes and physically fit Americans.

THE FUTURE

Finding the problems is easy; creating the solutions takes a little longer. AstroTurf® maintains a substantial research and development team at its plant in Dalton, Georgia. Each year the input of athletes, coaches, trainers, facilities managers, and administrators is included in efforts to meet today's and tomorrow's sports surfaces challenges. After almost 30 years the world of sports can look to AstroTurf® with confidence and trust in the Surface of Champions. . .AstroTurf®.

For more information about AstroTurf®, call 1/800/233-5714.

AstroTurf is a registered trademark of Southwest Recreational Industries, Inc.

Above: Opened in 1966, Busch Stadium is home to the successful St. Louis Cardinals and hosts almost 90 events each year, including high school and college football games, the circus, and concerts.

Top left: Home of the perennial Big Ten Conference contenders, Spartan Stadium hosts more than 200 events throughout the year. Since 1969 Michigan State University has installed three successive AstroTurf® fields, the most recent in 1994.

Left: The Toronto SkyDome, home of the back-to-back World Series Champions, the Toronto Bluejays, hosted 260 event days in 1994. Since its opening in 1989 more than 23 million people have attended events here, making it the most popular stadium in North America.

▶ Miller Brewing Company

MILLER BRINGS MORE THAN REFRESHMENT TO FANS AT PARK AND STADIUM EVENTS

Miller Brewing Company has a long tradition of supporting and adding value to sporting events and concerts in stadiums and ballparks across the country. Its ultimate objective is to increase fans' enjoyment of the event in a variety of ways. *The brewer's involvement begins in*

neighborhood stores and bars by providing fans with the game schedules (where legal) of local professional baseball, basketball, and football teams that are sponsored by Miller. These schedules list the home team's opponents, dates and times of each game, and are prepared both on posters with the name and emblem of the team and in free pocket-size guides.

For example, in advance of the football season, Miller offers a 40-page handbook that contains the complete NFL schedule for the year and includes team statistics, facts, and figures as well as the schedules of major college conferences. The handbook's circulation has grown to 15 million copies, which ranks it with *TV Guide* and makes the circulation of the Miller Lite NFL Football Handbook the largest of any football publication in the world.

For baseball fans, Miller creates free pocket cards with the schedules of the local teams that it sponsors. These quick references make it easy for sports fans to make advance plans to see a game.

FANS CAN WIN TICKETS AND TRIPS

To encourage even more interest, Miller Brewing Company often will sponsor promotions that give lucky consumers opportunities to win hard-to-get tickets to local sporting events or even attend playoff and championship games in other cities with free air travel, accommodations, and spending money, where legal, all courtesy of Miller.

At the actual games, Miller displays tasteful and attractive signs throughout the site, providing needed additional revenue for the park or stadium. Sometimes the support is direct, such as sponsorship of a scoreboard, or more general, such as being the major beer sponsor of the 1994 Super Bowl Game at the Georgia Dome. Miller also is one of the supporting sponsors of the Georgia Dome.

Where legal, fans who are 21 years of age or older also are treated to special Miller premium days during which they receive appropriate merchandise

such as floppy hats at baseball games or seat cushions at a football game.

But Miller goes beyond supporting established events. It also creates entertainment by sponsoring

tours of musical artists such as Brooks & Dunn, Page/Plant, and Emilio Navaira in ballparks and stadiums to accommodate thousands of concert-goers.

RESPONSIBLE DRINKING STRESSED

In another area, Miller Brewing Company works closely with the management of stadiums and ballparks to assure that fans drink responsibly. To this end, Miller and area distributors sponsor a variety of responsible-drinking programs that include distributing "Think When You Drink" buttons and sponsoring scoreboard messages to remind beer drinkers to drink responsibly.

Designated-driver and Safe Ride Home programs also are offered. In the designated-driver program, special booths are set up at a ballpark or stadium in conjunction with other sponsors. The person in a group who is 21 or older who agrees to be the designated driver is given a voucher for two free non-alchohol Miller Sharp's or soft drinks.

The Safe Ride Home program offers vouchers for free cab rides to fans who feel they are unable to drive home safely. They give the cab driver their car keys, which are returned when they reach home.

Miller also provides a program to concessionaires of alcohol beverages called Training for Intervention Procedures for Servers of alcohol, or TIPS. This program teaches servers how to encourage responsible drinking behavior through observation, evaluation, and intervention.

While the support and involvement of Miller Brewing Company has been praised by facility managers, sports teams, and performers, what is most appreciated by fans are the quality products Miller offers at these events. Joining friends for a hot dog and a refreshing cup of Miller beer adds to the enjoyment of any stadium or ballpark outing. It truly ranks among one of America's favorite traditions.

Miller Brewing Company creates free pocket cards with the schedules of such teams as the Pittsburgh Pirates, whose home stadium is Three Rivers. Photo by Dave Arrigo

▶ Contemporary Services Corporation

Contemporary Services Corporation is a full-service crowd management and event services and security organization. Since 1967 CSC has provided expertise in crowd management nationwide from regional offices throughout the United States. ➤ CSC provides state-of-the-art

CSC invented the peer group security concept, a middle-ground approach to crowd management now imitated by many other companies.

service in every phase of crowd management: security, parking, box office services, ticket taking, ushering, and even event maintenance—everything but concessions!

Peer group security, a middle-ground approach to crowd management, was invented by CSC. Peer group security is now imitated by many other companies, right down to CSC's trademark yellow jackets.

CSC is the largest entertainment service organization for premier stadiums across the United States. Its versatility and ability to offer custom-designed programs planned for specific venues and events has helped make CSC number one in the industry.

The firm has managed many of the biggest events in the country, including the Super Bowl and World Cup USA 1994 Soccer. CSC has managed the crowds at every Super Bowl since 1977, and was the only company to work at five different World Cup venues.

CSC has also managed crowds at many other events across the country, including stadium, arena, and amphitheater concerts; papal visits; professional and college football, basketball, baseball, and hockey; and every other conceivable private and public function. CSC's experience includes more than 500 stadium and more than 1,500 arena rock concerts. In addition to entertainment and sporting venues, CSC also provides traditional security guard service on a 24-hour basis at many city facilities, arenas, stadiums, hotels, and hospitals.

Clients of CSC include the NFL, NBA, NHL, Major

League Baseball, college football and basketball, and numerous musical concerts and tours, including the record-setting Jacksons Victory Tour, Elton John, the Rolling Stones, and the 1983 US Festival.

CSC's supervisors are among the most experienced and best educated in the field. With offices throughout the nation, CSC's full-time supervisors offer regional as well as national expertise.

Each of CSC's employees undergoes comprehensive training, from orientation to extensive briefings at every event. CSC hires the right personnel for the job—goal-oriented, self-motivated people with diverse backgrounds.

Directing CSC from its national headquarters in suburban Los Angeles are president Damon Zumwalt and vice president Peter Kranske. Zumwalt organized CSC in 1967 as a much-needed alternative to standard security systems. Zumwalt graduated from UCLA, where he was well known for his athletic and leadership skills. His innovative systems have made him a respected authority in his field as the pioneer of peer group security and crowd management. Kranske, also a former UCLA athlete, has experience in college football coaching, banking, and management. He is responsible for the planning of crowd management services for many major concerts and events, including every Super Bowl since Super Bowl XI and World Cup USA 1994 Soccer.

CSC has experienced managers and supervisors in over 20 branch offices serving more than 40 cities throughout the United States, including Colorado Springs, Denver, Ft. Collins, Fresno/Bakersfield, Jacksonville, Kansas City, Los Angeles/Long Beach/Orange County, Memphis, Miami/Ft. Lauderdale, Nashville, New Orleans, Orlando, Phoenix, Pittsburgh, Raleigh, St. Louis, Salt Lake City/Park City, San Antonio, San Diego, San Francisco/San Jose/Oakland, Santa Barbara/Ventura/Oxnard, Santa Rosa, Seattle/Tacoma, Tampa/St. Petersburg, Tucson, and Washington, D.C./Baltimore.

For information regarding CSC, call 800/754-5150.

▶ Covermaster Inc.

"With Covermaster® you're always ahead of the game," says Bob Curry, president of Covermaster Inc. of Rexdale, Ontario. It's a slogan that's literally true of a company that supplies stadiums around the world with an amazing variety of protective sports surfaces covers.

Back in 1969 the firm rented tarps to the trucking and construction industries. "Business was good," recalls Bob, "but we quickly set our sights on bigger and better projects. With rock concerts on the rise, stadium managers needed special field protection to allow their facilities to be converted for multi-use. We entered the field with large-size neoprene tarps for use on artificial turf, followed by nonwoven, needle-punched geotextile covers for grass."

However, with ever bigger crowds, huge stages, enormous sound systems, trucks and special seating, grass repairs became time-consuming and costly. This led Covermaster to AKZO NOBEL Geosynthetics Company of Asheville, North Carolina, a manufacturer of synthetic fibers and developer of a special matting for erosion control that, when slightly modified, proved to be ideal for use on top of the grass as well.

They called this grass protection cover Enkamat® Flatback. It's made of a geomatrix design of interwoven nylon monofilaments that are fused where they intersect to create an open mesh-type matting. Just imagine bunched up, heavy fishing line and you get the picture. For added strength, the upper layer of the filaments was flattened. Voilà—a strong natural grass cover that lets plenty of light, air, and moisture through for use over extended periods.

AKZO began using Enkamat under the surface to reinforce grass soccer fields in Europe. In the late 1970s the same technology was introduced to the United States as Enkaturf®. Enkaturf has been used successfully in high schools, colleges, and countless golf course applications, in high-profile fields such as the Rose Bowl, Grambling University, Purdue University, New Mexico State, and in NFL stadiums such as the Orange Bowl and Candlestick Park.

With Covermaster's long-standing experience, AKZO appointed the company as distributor of Enkamat Flatback to sports facilities in North and South America. Cleveland Municipal Stadium was the first to test the new cover. Today many stadiums use Enkamat, including Soldier Field, RFK, and Anaheim.

With the trend away from artificial turf—of the 28 NFL franchises, 13 now use grass instead of just 11 in the late 1980s—and with the World Cup Soccer games proving that grass can be used indoors, Enkamat and Enkaturf are poised to help promote the continued use of grass fields as we move into the twenty-first century.

For quick grass repairs, Covermaster's Evergreen cover is the one to use. Ideal also for late season sodding and longer root development, Evergreen creates a greenhouse effect. Moisture and light get through while some daytime warmth is trapped. Evergreen is a groundskeeper's delight and now very much a standard tool, particularly at facilities located in the transitional zone and colder climates.

The company also supplies custom products. For instance, for the SkyDome in Toronto, Rich Stadium in Buffalo, and others, Covermaster developed high quality, custom designed wall padding that meets specific needs in baseball and football situations.

Covermaster offers protection against the elements as well. We're talking about the AFC 460 lightweight, heat reflective, baseball raincover, and football fieldcover. At half the price of conventional covers, it is the most widely used raincover in North America today.

Covermaster's commitment to the stadium industry is simple. "We strive to meet their needs, come what may." For Covermaster, keeping the customer satisfied and happy is more than a business approach, it's a way of life!

Above: Workers roll out Enkamat Flatback protective cover at Cleveland Municipal Stadium to set up for a concert.

Top: Covermaster engineered, manufactured, and installed custom wall padding at SkyDome Stadium in Toronto.

For more information, call:
(Toll-free) 800/387-5808 or 416/745-1811
Fax: 416/742-6837
Or write to:
100 Westmore Drive, 11-D
Rexdale, Ontario M9V5C3

▶ Jacobsen Division of Textron Inc.

JACOBSEN TURF EQUIPMENT AT GREAT SPORTS FIELDS ACROSS NORTH AMERICA

Ask any true baseball fan for a short list of favorite Major League Baseball stadiums and, without a doubt, Boston's Fenway Park will be near the top. ⚑ Ask any college football fan for the same thing, and while many great stadiums are filled to capacity with exciting

Soldier Field set against one of the world's most famous skylines.

Eric Adkins, assistant director of golf for the Chicago Park District, created the unique circular mowing pattern for the World Cup games at Soldier Field using a Jacobsen LF-100 lightweight fairway mower.

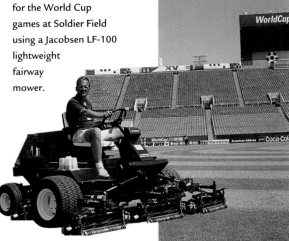

tradition, the Rose Bowl in Pasadena, California, is the granddaddy of them all.

Fenway Park and the Rose Bowl, two of the great sports stadiums in North America, are rich in heritage. And they are two of the many great sports fields maintained with Jacobsen turf maintenance equipment.

Jacobsen products are renowned for their high quality of cut. Jacobsen equipment is in use on 75 percent of the world's golf courses, and more courses trust their valuable greens and fairways to Jacobsen products than to any other manufacturer.

Great sports fields trust their turf to Jacobsen for the same reason great golf courses do—Jacobsen leaves beautiful turf looking its best.

In 1921 Knud Jacobsen, a Danish immigrant, founded the Jacobsen Manufacturing Company in Racine, Wisconsin. He and his partners designed and built the 4-Acre, the first motorized reel mower with an engine specifically designed for a lawn mower. The 4-Acre was aptly named, as it was capable of cutting four acres a day.

Over the years Jacobsen has led the turf care industry with innovative, quality products. The company introduced the first hydraulically powered riding greens mower, the Greens King, in 1969. In the 1980s Jacobsen introduced the LF-100, a lightweight fairway mower, and changed forever the way golf courses care for their fairways.

The same Jacobsen products that create beautiful turf on the world's most beautiful golf courses create world-class turf on the great sports fields of North America.

During the 1994 World Cup, Jacobsen equipment maintained the turf at seven of the nine stadiums hosting World Cup games, including the natural turf installed indoors at the Pontiac Silverdome near Detroit.

The revolutionary Silverdome field was maintained with Jacobsen Greens King IV greens mowers equipped with seven-blade reels. Greens King IV mowers were also used at the Rose Bowl, site of the World Cup final and one semifinal game, and at Giants Stadium at the Meadowlands, East Rutherford, New Jersey, site of the other World Cup semifinal.

At Soldier Field in Chicago, where five first-round World Cup matches were played, Eric Adkins created a unique circular mowing pattern with a Jacobsen LF-100. Adkins, the assistant director of golf for the Chicago Park District, was well aware of the LF-100's capabilities. The LF-100 creates the beautiful striping effect found on top golf courses around the world.

At Dodger Stadium in Los Angeles and Jack Murphy Stadium in San Diego, Jacobsen Greens King IV greens mowers equipped with Jacobsen's patented Turf Groomer turf conditioners keep the field in perfect condition. Turf Groomers help eliminate grain that can cause the baseball to snake, or change direction, as it rolls through the grass. A truer roll allows players to be more aggressive when fielding ground balls.

Whether the sport is baseball, football, or soccer, Bowls of Glory and Fields of Dreams across North America demand beautiful turf—beautiful turf from Jacobsen.

Jacobsen Division of Textron Inc. is a major manufacturer of professional turf maintenance equipment used worldwide.

▶ Lithonia Lighting

The largest lighting equipment manufacturer in North America, Lithonia

Lighting provides single-source responsibility for all stadium lighting

requirements, from downlighting for suites, restaurants, and common

areas to outdoor fixtures and poles for parking lots and walkways.

Lithonia also has the exits, emergency signs, and control systems required throughout the facility and the fluorescent parabolics for offices.

And, of course, Lithonia Lighting offers the best value in sports lighting—from fixtures for Little League ballparks to systems for multimillion-dollar stadiums.

ARENAVISION

Lithonia has teamed up with Philips Lighting Corporation to bring ArenaVision, today's most advanced sports and event lighting system, to North America. In use throughout Europe, ArenaVision was developed by Philips and is marketed in North America exclusively by Lithonia Lighting.

ArenaVision ensures that spectators, players, and television viewers enjoy clear visibility and perfect color without glare. ArenaVision fixtures provide superior light output from all viewing angles, delivering the studio-quality key, fill, and backlighting critical to high-definition television requirements. The sharp cutoff optics also reduce disturbing light spill from the stadium.

Smaller than conventional fixtures, ArenaVision allows optimum flexibility in arena and stadium design. Slimmer masts and headframes can be used, and there is more opportunity for roof or gallery mounting.

To ensure that ArenaVision meets all requirements, Lithonia offers a wide range of options—from an external visor to a battery back-up. Other available options enhance drama and excitement; these include hot restrike, a long-range ignitor, and a dimming circuit.

ARENA LIGHTING CONTROLS

Complementing ArenaVision is the Arena Lighting Control System. This centralized PC-based control system is designed for indoor or outdoor multipurpose venues. All lighting in the arena is configured instantly by pressing a single button or selecting a

Lithonia Lighting offers the best value in stadium lighting.

preset on the PC screen. Custom interactive graphics simplify programming, and software access is limited by multilevel security. In addition, one-time lighting scenes for special events are easy to develop.

Since maintenance is a key consideration for large-scale lighting systems, lamp life of all fixtures is monitored automatically. This permits relamping before lamp failures compromise an event.

RECENT PROJECTS

Recent Lithonia Lighting projects include Delta Center, home of the Utah Jazz and the Salt Lake Golden Eagles; Target Center, home of the Minnesota Timberwolves; and the Georgia Dome, home of the Atlanta Falcons. Worldwide, ArenaVision was used in venues built for the Barcelona Summer Olympics and seven of the last 10 World Cup championships. The new Cerbantes Stadium in St. Louis and the refurbished Soldier Field in Chicago also feature ArenaVision.

*C*incinnati's Riverfront Stadium
on the Ohio River is home to the
NFL Bengals. Photo by James Blank /
Scenics of America

NFL STADIUMS

Stadium + Franchise = Bonanza

After decades of tolerating hand-me-down baseball parks, overaged municipal stadiums, college gridirons of debatable merit, and even high school fields, National Football League fans, players, and others in the pro football constituency are coming into their own. Fans are getting surroundings and creature comforts they feel they deserve for an average NFL ticket price of $31. Increasingly, players are getting the kinds of locker, training, and medical facilities more in keeping with an average salary in excess of $700,000.

Spurred by more than one billion dollars in television revenues and total TV audience of 80 million, NFL franchises are building new stadiums, renovat-

Right: Artificial turf covers the playing field in Giants Stadium in East Rutherford, New Jersey. The stadium can accommodate 77,000 spectators for football games. Courtesy, Meadowlands Arena/Giants Stadium, New Jersey Sports & Exposition Authority

Far right: Until recently the 70-plus-year-old Los Angeles Memorial Coliseum was the oldest stadium in use by the NFL. Today college football's USC Trojans call the Coliseum home. Photo by James Blank / Scenics of America

ing existing ones, or letting it be known that they are willing to pick up and move to a city ready to provide a new stadium.

It wasn't always this way. Since the league's inception in 1919, NFL teams had to catch as catch can. The New England Patriots are a case in point. The Pats, who began as the Boston Patriots, played their first two seasons (1960-1962) in Nickerson Field, Boston University's home turf. The next stop (1963-1968) was Fenway Park, home of the Boston Red Sox. In 1969 the Pats played at Alumni Stadium on Boston's College's Chestnut Hill campus. The following year the team moved to the venerable Harvard Stadium before settling in at Foxboro Stadium (previously known as Sullivan Stadium and, before that, Schaefer Stadium) in 1972.

As of May 1995, 28 NFL franchises played in 8 open-air, football-only stadiums, 6 domes, and 10 multipurpose outdoor stadiums of varying ages and conditions. The newest NFL stadium in current use is the Georgia Dome, built in 1992 for the Atlanta Falcons. The Los Angeles Memorial Coliseum, built in 1923 to house the 1932 Olympics, was the oldest NFL stadium in use until recently.

This picture will change significantly before the end of the decade. Five years ago the average life expectancy of a pro football stadium would be in excess of 75 years. Now, however, with the new franchise costs and ever-changing revenue streams sought by NFL owners, that

average age has been reduced to about 30 years before extensive renovations or new construction will be required again. The move by the Rams from aging Anaheim Stadium to a brand new domed stadium in St. Louis was the signal for a series of announcements of contemplated venue changes by NFL teams. The NFL Raiders and Chicago Bears are working toward playing in new stadiums even if that means moving to new cities, while the Tampa Bay Buccaneers are seeking greener pastures to replace the 28-year-old Tampa Stadium. As the 1995 season opened, the Cleveland Browns and

Cincinnati Bengals, seeking alternatives to Cleveland Stadium and Riverfront Stadium, have expressed an interest in moving to Los Angeles to fill the void left by the Rams' and Raiders' departure.

The NFL's two newest expansion franchises, the Carolina Panthers and the Jacksonville Jaguars, will play in open-air, natural turf, football-only stadiums with a full range of practice, training, and medical facilities. The Panthers are building privately financed

The Colts play their home games in the RCA Dome in Indianapolis. Courtesy, Indiana Convention Center

73,000-seat Carolinas Stadium in uptown Charlotte. The Jaguars will make their debut in 1995 in a totally renovated, municipally financed 73,000-seat Gator Bowl.

The bringing of the Panthers' Carolinas Stadium to Charlotte is a casebook study of what's involved in designing, promoting, and building an NFL stadium for the mid-1990s. Along with other franchises, it also provides a preview of the future role and direction of NFL stadiums.

Panthers chairman Jerry Richardson and son Mark, who is general manager, chose Charlotte, North Carolina, as the home of a regional franchise with a pool of 10 million people within a radius of 150 miles. Jerry Richardson, who played for the Baltimore Colts and then built a fortune in the fast-food business, has the background and resources to manage an NFL franchise. The Richard-

sons pushed all the right buttons to cultivate support for a stadium.

They chose private financing over government funding because, says stadium operations director Jon Richardson (Mark's brother), "We wanted to give something back to the Carolinas, and we didn't want taxpayers to foot the bill."

They made Carolinas Stadium urban, situating it on 33 acres in Charlotte's uptown district. The location is convenient to an expected 4,600 hotel rooms and 52 restaurants.

They spared no cost in designing a premier quality stadium, called by Mark Richardson, "the most perfect single-purpose facility possible." Scoreboard, replay board, public address system, and lighting are state of the art. Creature comforts are far ahead of the curve, with a concession stand for every 178 seats (instead of one per 300 spectators, the current norm for the NFL) and 68 rest rooms, equally divided between men's and women's facilities.

Finally, they targeted the Charlotte area's large and prosperous business and banking community by offering for sale 135 luxury suites and 10,000 club seats. Season ticket purchasers at every level were also required to buy permanent seat licenses (PSLs), which guarantee lifetime rights to a stadium seat as a precondition of buying a season ticket.

The Panthers silenced skeptics, including many NFL owners, by selling more than 50,000 PSLs at prices ranging from $600 to $5,400. More than 20,000 of those seats were sold the day they went on sale, yielding a one-day cash take of $41 million. The PSL sales, which are over and above the price of a season ticket, *netted* $100 million of the stadium's $160-million price tag. The remainder of the money came from private investors. To reinforce the fans' sense of inclusion in the development of Carolinas Stadium, the names of the first 25,000 PSL buyers will be engraved in a "wall of fame" planned for the stadium's entry area.

The Richardsons are also building a strong identity between the franchise and the

The Stadiums and Ballparks of the NFL

AMERICAN FOOTBALL CONFERENCE

CLUB	STADIUM	SEATS	SURFACE	YEAR BUILT
Buffalo Bills	Rich Stadium	80,000	Artificial	1973
Cincinnati Bengals	Riverfront Stadium	60,000	Artificial	1970
Cleveland Browns	Cleveland Stadium	78,500	Grass	1931
Denver Broncos	Mile High Stadium	76,000	Grass	1948
Houston Oilers	Astrodome	62,000	Artificial	1965
Indianapolis Colts	RCA Dome	60,000	Artificial	1983
Kansas City Chiefs	Arrowhead Stadium	70,000	Grass	1972
Los Angeles Raiders*	Los Angeles Coliseum	92,500	Grass	1923
Miami Dolphins	Joe Robbie Stadium	73,000	Grass	1987
New England Patriots	Foxboro Stadium	61,000	Grass	1971
New York Jets	Giants Stadium	77,000	Artificial	1976
Pittsburgh Steelers	Three Rivers Stadium	60,000	Artificial	1970
San Diego Chargers	Jack Murphy Stadium	60,000	Grass	1967
Seattle Seahawks	Kingdome	66,400	Artificial	1976

NATIONAL FOOTBALL CONFERENCE

CLUB	STADIUM	SEATS	SURFACE	YEAR BUILT
Atlanta Falcons	Georgia Dome	70,500	Artificial	1992
Carolina Panthers	Carolinas Stadium	73,200	Grass	1996
Chicago Bears	Soldier Field	67,000	Grass	1924
Dallas Cowboys	Texas Stadium	65,000	Artificial	1971
Detroit Lions	Pontiac Silverdome**	80,000	Artificial	1975
Green Bay Packers	Lambeau Field	57,000	Grass	1957
Jacksonville Jaguars	To be named	73,800	Grass	1995
Minnesota Vikings	Humphrey Metrodome	63,000	Artificial	1982
New Orleans Saints	Louisiana Superdome	69,000	Artificial	1975
New York Giants	Giants Stadium	77,000	Artificial	1976
Philadelphia Eagles	Veterans Stadium	65,000	Artificial	1971
Phoenix Cardinals	Sun Devil Stadium	73,000	Grass	1958
St. Louis Rams	The Domed Stadium at America's Center	70,000	Artificial	1995
San Francisco 49ers	Candlestick Park	66,500	Grass	1960
Tampa Bay Bucs	Tampa Stadium	74,000	Grass	1967
Washington Redskins	RFK Stadium	56,000	Grass	1961

*Information current as of May 1995. Team name and stadium subject to change.
**The Pontiac Silverdome is the only domed stadium built solely for football.

A capacity crowd of
60,000 filled San Diego
Jack Murphy Stadium for
this Chargers game.
Photo by James Blank /
Scenics of America

stadium—even before the team has been formed. Says Dennis Wellner, who designs NFL stadiums for the HOK Sports Facilities Group of Kansas City, Missouri: "Mark Richardson made his philosophy clear. He wanted more than a place for his team to play. He told us he wanted a *home* for his team. That's an important distinction, and it resonates with the fans, the players and the community."

Max Muhleman, the sports marketing consultant instrumental in bringing NFL and NBA teams to Charlotte, says that by building a well-heeled fan base, identifying heavily with the Carolinas, and referring to Carolinas Stadium as a home for the Panthers, the Richardsons are creating a potentially powerful franchise/stadium synergy. Muhleman describes that synergy with the following equation: Stadium + Franchise = Bonanza. "The Dallas Cowboys and Texas Stadium built that kind of synergy long ago," says Muhleman. "Now they're a sports superpower." Team and stadium were joined forever in the public mind when Cowboys fans bragged that Texas Stadium was built with a hole in its roof so "God could watch his favorite team play."

At the same time as new stadiums are being built or contemplated, older stadiums are undergoing or planning extensive face-lifts and expansions. Some examples include the Gator Bowl in Jacksonville, Florida; Arrowhead Stadium in Kansas City, Missouri; Joe Robbie Stadium in Miami, Florida; Don Hutson Center in Green Bay, Wisconsin; and Texas Stadium in Arlington, Texas.

The expansion Jacksonville Jaguars opened in August 1995 in a totally reconstructed, publicly funded Gator Bowl that, except for its west upper deck, will bear no resemblance to the original. The $109-million project includes virtually total demolition of the entire Gator Bowl. Pro games will seat 73,000, college games 82,000. Like Carolinas Stadium, the Gator Bowl will have three adjacent practice fields.

Kansas City's Arrowhead Stadium, built

in 1972 as the NFL's first pro football-only stadium, switched from artificial to natural turf for the 1994 season and added two video boards, a game-in-progress board, and more than 1,000 seats. Among new amenities for Chiefs players are: a new weight room, expanded home team locker rooms (visiting team amenities are kept to a minimum), and position-by-position breakout rooms for coach-player meetings. The media get a 120-person auditorium for press conferences and additional television locations.

Miami's Joe Robbie Stadium, the Dolphins' home field since 1987, has embarked on a three-year, $25-million renovation program that includes the addition of two elevators, a parking lot expansion, resurfacing all concourses, painting all walls, upgrading lighting and sound systems, and a new video screen on the east-end scoreboard. An additional creature comfort: cup holders on all seats.

The Green Bay Packers in 1994 opened the Don Hutson Center (named for the Packers' legendary Hall of Fame end), a 2.5-acre, 112,000-square-foot indoor practice facility adjoining Lambeau Field. The two practice fields in the Center have 85- and 90-foot ceilings for punting and field goal practice.

On the drawing board at the Dallas Cowboys' Texas Stadium: A plan to raise the roof to accommodate an additional 40,000-seat deck, bringing the stadium's total number of seats to 105,000, the most in the NFL.

Anyone looking at the spate of NFL

stadium building and renovation going on today could not be blamed for asking what took so long. Well, while the league has existed since 1919, pro football really didn't catch on until the 1960s and network television coverage. While college teams filled the mammoth stadiums of the Big Ten and the Southeast Conference, the pros toiled before sparse crowds in catch-as-catch-can accommodations. Divisions and conferences were impermanent, and franchises were nomadic. It wasn't until the emergence of mediagenic stars such as Otto Graham, Elroy Hirsch,

Frank Gifford, Bob Waterfield, and Night Train Lane that NFL players caught the public's fancy. The early NFL stars attracted TV, and TV made a star of the NFL.

Compared with the tens of millions of people watching NFL football on TV on any given Sunday, 70,000 fans in a stadium's seats equates to a few close friends dropping by for a drink. So why all the emphasis on upgrading pro football's stadium stock? There are several reasons:

• *Cash flow.* At an average admission price of

(Text continues on page 124)

NFL Stadiums: The Stars Remember the Way They Were

Pampered playing surfaces and sumptuous amenities for players might rate a top priority in today's NFL stadiums, but they didn't always. To appreciate how far National Football League stadiums have come, ponder the recollections of some NFL veterans of the 1960s and 1970s, when most pro football was played in baseball parks, over-aged municipal stadiums, college gridirons, and even high school fields.

Hall of Fame quarterback Len Dawson began his pro career playing for the Pittsburgh Steelers in Forbes Field, a baseball park where, he recalls, there wasn't a good seat in the house for football and where the turf was worn down to bedrock by daily practices as well as Sunday games. He once played an entire football game on a tarp that froze to the playing field after a snow storm. "It was a toss-up as to which was worse, the tarp or the field," says Dawson.

Before starring with the Washington Redskins, NFL Hall of Famer Sonny Jurgensen plied the quarterback's trade with the Philadelphia Eagles at Franklin Field, which was built in 1895 and claims the dubious distinction of being America's oldest football stadium. "Franklin switched to an early version of artificial turf in 1969, and it has a hump as high as a pitcher's mound that ran the length of the field for drainage," says

Sam Huff, Hall of Fame linebacker.

Jurgensen. "If you sat on one sideline bench, you couldn't see over the hump to the opposite sideline," he says, "And if I threw a sideline pass, I had to aim it down, like a baseball pitcher, or it went over the receiver's head."

Jan Stenerud was an all-pro placekicker in constant search of a level playing field, or at least a few feet of one, on which to plant his non-kicking leg. He harbors particularly nasty memories of Shea Stadium's rutted, unkempt turf. "It was especially bad in 1969 after the Mets won the World Series and the fans tore up the field," Stennerud says.

Former Cleveland Browns running back and special teams player Greg Pruitt winces at the memory of the frozen surface of Cleveland Stadium. Says Pruitt, " I used to say, let's play in the parking lot. At least we *know* it's concrete."

It's a rare NFL veteran who doesn't have horror stories of

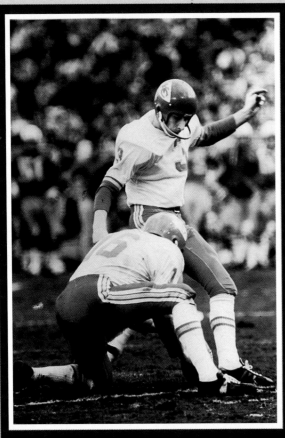

All-pro place-kicker Jan Stenerud.

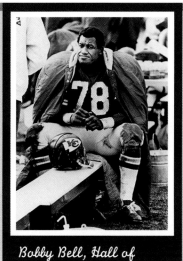

Bobby Bell, Hall of Fame linebacker.

COURTESY, KANSAS CITY CHIEFS

cramped, dank stadium locker rooms with dangerously slippery floors and, often, no hot water for showers.

Because so many NFL games were played in baseball parks, players had to use locker facilities designed for baseball teams, whose members were fewer in number, smaller in size, and wore far less gear than the voluminously padded and armored football players.

Hall of Fame linebacker Bobby Bell says Baltimore Memorial Stadium's locker room was so puny that the players had to change in shifts. Pruitt uses the word "incarcerated" to describe how he felt in the Houston Astrodome's cramped locker facilities.

Stennerud worried more about getting hurt on slick, bare locker room floors than on the playing field.

Between the treacherous playing fields and the substandard locker rooms lay another peril—hostile fans. Robert Jackson, an all-pro offensive guard for the Cleveland Browns, shudders at the memory of a chain link fence being all that separated him from snarling home-team partisans in Oakland-Alameda County Coliseum. Pruitt tells of an overzealous Denver fan running up behind the Cleveland bench, snatching a teammate's helmet,

and tossing it into the stands at Mile High Stadium. Bobby Bell says he sought postgame protection from hostile fans by trotting into the locker room tunnel next to home-team players. "The guys on the other team didn't know it, but they were my body guards," says Bell.

The rigorous conditions found in older stadiums are not without their defenders among former NFL stars. Robert Jackson says Cleveland Stadium's gnarled frozen surface gave him an advantage at his position of offensive guard. Says he, "I was able to dig in to make my block, while the defensive ends weren't

Greg Pruitt, former Cleveland Browns running back and special teams player.

COURTESY, THE CLEVELAND BROWNS

sure of their footing when they made their rush."

Hall of Fame linebacker Sam Huff maintains that a stadium's culture and tradition compensate for its material shortcomings. "I loved playing in Yankee Stadium because it's the most famous stadium in the world, he says. "I was using the same locker room and playing on the same field as Lou Gehrig, Mickey Mantle, and Yogi Berra." Huff

also remembers the much-maligned Cleveland Stadium fondly. "Sure it's cold and noisy and the field can be bad, but I loved it because I knew I'd be facing Jim Brown, the greatest running back who ever lived," he says, adding this John Maddenesque note: "Football players shouldn't be too comfortable," says Huff. "Being cold, muddy, and dirty and playing on frozen fields are all part of the game."

For today's players, stadium steam rooms, weight rooms, saunas, and lap pools are also part of the game. Comparing today's facilities with those of his rookie year, Len Dawson says, "Today's players don't know how good they have it." Bobby Bell claims that if today's conditions had existed 20 years ago, he would still be playing at age 54. Each could have added that it was he and the other stars of his era who made possible today's comfortable, well-equipped NFL stadiums by making pro football America's favorite spectator sport.

$30, 70,000 fans bring in $2.1 million per game, or $21 million for a home schedule of two preseason and eight regular-season games. Assuming that 80 percent of fans hold season tickets, the franchise can get $17 million up front.

- *Image.* Every NFL franchise recognizes the importance of the "blimp factor," or how its stadium looks on TV from 1,000 feet up. The crowd is as much a part of the show as the game for the TV audience and for the spectators. A jammed stadium says this is a successful franchise, even if the team did lose its last four games. Blocks of empty seats send the opposite message. The overhead blimp shot also gives the stadium a community context. Jeff Klein, Director of Stadium Operations for the Kansas City Chiefs, points out that Arrowhead Stadium is Kansas City's geographical landmark because, he says, "We don't have an Arch [as in St. Louis] or a Statue of Liberty."

- *Repeat business.* Enough chewing gum on the seats, cold hot dogs, or rest room lines that last halfway through the third quarter of the game and you've given fans reasons to trade in their stadium seats for their living room couches.

- *Grass roots support.* For all its TV-driven national and, increasingly, international appeal, all NFL football, like politics, is local. Grass-roots support for franchise and stadium is essential, especially when the stadium is publicly funded. Owners, coaches, and players must continually lobby civic, cultural, political, and business leaders.

By now it's a rare NFL stadium that isn't engaged in some kind of renovation or rebuilding. Are we likely to witness the evolution of a traditional NFL stadium design template? Is an NFL stadium "look" emerging? Will there be a standard NFL stadium design? Stadium architects and sports marketing consultants think not. "Each successful NFL stadium reflects the highly individualized character of its team, its ownership, its fans, its community and its market, and these vary wildly around the country," says stadium architect Dennis Wellner. Neither is there a trend in stadium design and construction to parallel the wave of nostalgia that has set the tone for the new wave of baseball stadiums, quite possibly because NFL fans can't find any old stadiums to feel nostalgic about.

One reason for the diverse design and construction of NFL stadiums is that NFL football fits into different markets in different ways. For example, despite the bad-mouthing of domes by stadium purists, Colts games at the RCA Dome in Indianapolis are a selling point for adjacent hospitality and convention facilities. St. Louis attracted the Rams to a 70,000-seat domed stadium that will be an extension of an urban convention center.

The same could be said for the playing surface issue. While the demonization of artificial turf continues, highly respected facilities such as Texas Stadium, Giants Stadium, and Buffalo's Rich Stadium continue with it. Giants Stadium disappointed grass-stadium partisans when it took up the sod laid down for the World Cup in 1994 and went back to AstroTurf.

Old or still under construction, an NFL stadium is indeed a reflection of the spirit of its franchise, community, and the personality and philosophy of its team, coaches, owners, and fans. The Richardsons are making sure that an upscale, fan-friendly Carolinas Stadium will set the tone for the franchise until the Panthers establish their bona fides on the playing field. Antediluvian, icy, noisy Cleveland Stadium, where Jim Brown trampled tacklers, Paul Brown called all the plays, and Lou Groza kicked soaring field goals, is quintessential hard-bitten Cleveland. The Packers' Lambeau Field in Green Bay is where Vince Lombardi's ghost walks. Phil Pionek, executive assistant to the president of the Green Bay Packers, says that the franchise is constantly reminded that it must keep up with the times by adding private suites and club seating. "But no matter how modern we get," he says, "we never lose touch with our heritage."

▶ RFK Memorial Stadium

Surely Pierre-Charles L'Enfant envisioned the gleaming white concrete, aluminum, glass, and marble of the Robert F. Kennedy Memorial Stadium, in the shadow of the capitol, as the eastern most landmark to terminate the long sweep of open spaces and magnificent buildings that were

a part of his main plan for Washington—a swath through the city's center that starts in the west with the Lee Mansion and Arlington Cemetery and includes the Lincoln Memorial, and the Washington Monument.

Of the many potential sites studied, 160 acres of government-owned land at the foot of East Capitol Street offered the advantage of fitting into L'Enfant's plan of the city. In 1957 Representative Oren Harris of Arkansas introduced the D.C. Stadium Act of 1957. Ground breaking for the stadium commenced on July 8, 1960.

On October 7, 1961, the stadium was dedicated as the "District of Columbia Stadium" with a football match-up between George Washington University and Virginia Military Institute. The Redskins played their first season at the stadium that same year, leaving the crumbling wooden relic known as Griffith Stadium behind. The District of Columbia Stadium easily took its place as one of the leading architectural and engineering marvels of its day, ranking among the largest in the world and as the second-largest Major League stadium in the United States. This almost perfectly circular building was heralded for having "no bad seats in the house."

In the spring of 1962 the "new" Washington Senators (an expanded team that replaced the "old" Senators who had moved north to become the Minnesota Twins) arrived and began play with President John F. Kennedy throwing out the first pitch.

Ironically, in June 1969 the District of Columbia Stadium was renamed the Robert F. Kennedy Memorial Stadium (RFK) after President Kennedy's assassinated brother.

From 1961 to 1971 the stadium was home to both the Redskins and the Senators. However, in 1972, the Senators departed for Texas, leaving the Stadium with only one major tenant, the Redskins. It has also been the home of some of the world's greatest coaches, among them the Redskins' Vince Lombardi, George Allen, and Joe Gibbs. Notable athletes who have suited up at RFK for the Redskins include Sonny Jurgenson, Sam Huff, Bobby Mitchell, Charley Taylor, Larry Brown, Billy Kilmer, and Joe Theismann.

Over its nearly 35-year history, RFK has been host to a wide variety of events. More U.S. presidents have attended events here than any other stadium in America. It was an early stop for the Beatles and was host to opening night for the Rolling Stones' worldwide tour in 1994. A world heavyweight title fight was held at RFK in 1993 and in 1994, when the United States hosted the World Cup Soccer tournament, RFK was the site of five of those games.

Today, with a seating capacity of 56,000-plus, RFK continues to host many major events in the nation's capital. Its comfort, ease of access, and electric atmosphere have endured, making RFK an important venue in the sports and entertainment field.

Left: RFK Memorial Stadium hosted five 1994 World Cup Soccer games. Photo by Regis Lefebure

Above: The stadium is home to the Washington Redskins. Photo by Regis Lefebure

▶ Giants Stadium

Giants Stadium, located in East Rutherford, New Jersey, is an integral part of the Meadowlands Sports Complex. Along with the Meadowlands Racetrack and Byrne Meadowlands Arena, it is owned and operated by the New Jersey Sports and Exposition Authority. Giants Stadium is the only stadium in the United States that is home to two professional football teams—the Giants and the Jets of the National Football League.

The Giants, for whom the stadium is named, opened the stadium on October 10, 1976, while the Jets began playing regular season games in 1984. Other professional franchises that have called Giants

More football games are played each year at Giants Stadium than at any other stadium in the country.

Stadium home include the New Jersey Generals of the United States Football League, the New York/New Jersey Knights of the World League of American Football, and the Cosmos of the North American Soccer League, which featured the renowned Pele.

The stadium is also host to college football. Prominent among the games are the Kickoff Classic, traditionally the first game played each year, Rutgers/Big East, and the Army-Navy game. All in all, approximately 25 football games are played in the stadium each year, far exceeding any other stadium in the country.

Giants Stadium has been the scene of other significant and exciting events, including the closing ceremonies of the 1986 Statue of Liberty Rededication Week, seven 1994 World Cup Soccer games, including a semifinal, and a visit by Pope John Paul II in October 1995. In addition, the stadium has been the site of many major concerts and is the primary choice of promoters in the metropolitan area. A record-setting 15 concerts were performed in 1994 alone.

Designed by Hellmuth, Obata and Kassabaum's Sports Facilities Group (HOK Sport), Giants Stadium is situated, along with its sister facilities, on 750 acres that include 25,000 parking spaces. Total seating capacity is 77,716, which is distributed over three levels. The stadium was built with the fan in mind—the seats are close to the action and the sightlines are excellent with absolutely no obstructions. Seventy-two luxury suites and a spacious two-level press box are situated on the mezzanine level. There are four gates, which have a total of 56 ticket windows and 80 turnstiles. Eight spiral ramps and 24 escalators, eight of which travel to each level, allow easy ingress and egress. Seventy restrooms and 40 permanent concession stands assist in patron comfort.

The playing surface is normally 110,000 square feet of artificial turf, but for the 1994 World Cup games a Bermuda sod field was installed over the turf. As a result of the success of the grass field during World Cup, discussions have taken place regarding the conversion from artificial turf to natural grass. This is one of several possible stadium renovations that may occur in the near future. Also on the drawing board are the addition of 104 luxury suites and a sound system upgrade.

Giants Stadium is a state-of-the-art facility that boasts the most dedicated and professional staff in the business. Its success is driven and acknowledged by its loyal patrons, 36 million of whom have passed through its doors since opening. If it's excitement you want, then Giants Stadium is the place to be.

▶ Tampa Stadium

Built in 1967, Tampa Stadium was designed to be home for the

University of Tampa football team (now disbanded) and other college

games. Community leaders had bigger plans for the stadium, however,

and on August 10, 1968, began fulfilling those visions by watching the

Washington Redskins beat the Atlanta Falcons 16-14 in the stadium's first NFL exhibition game.

The stadium became home to the NFL's Tampa Bay Buccaneers in 1975, and underwent a $10-million renovation that included the expansion of seating from 47,000 to 72,000, the addition of sky suites, and the enclosing of the end zones.

After four short seasons, in 1979 the Buccaneers fell one game short of the Super Bowl, losing to the Los Angeles Rams, 9-0.

Notable events held at Tampa Stadium include Super Bowl XVIII and the USFL Championship, in 1984; the first of 10 Hall of Fame Bowls, in 1987; and Super Bowl XXV, held during Operation Desert Storm, in 1991. Fans were enthralled by Whitney Houston's heart-rending rendition of *The Star Spangled Banner*. General Norman Schwartzkopf and the U.S. troops were honored in May 1992 as the stadium hosted the first homecoming celebration for its hometown hero. Important annual events held at the stadium include the Florida Classic (the state's oldest and longest uninterrupted football rivalry and the nation's second-largest African-American football classic) and the American Invitational of Horse Jumping (the U.S. national championship).

In addition to hosting pro and college football games, Tampa Stadium is a multiuse facility that sees dozens of high school games, soccer games, concerts, festivals, motor sports shows, sales seminars, equestrian events, and dog shows each year.

Tampa Stadium has instituted several exceptional programs for its guests, including Tag-A-Kid,

Tampa Stadium is home to the NFL's Buccaneers.

designed to assist parents of young children while attending events on stadium property; Safe Ride Home, a safety precaution that offers free taxi rides home to attendees who have consumed too much alcohol; and a comprehensive recycling program that encourages fans to participate by bringing their tailgating recyclables to designated stadium gate locations.

GREATEST MOMENTS IN TAMPA STADIUM HISTORY

Super Bowl XVIII
Most rushing yards gained in a single SB game
Marcus Allen, Raiders, 191
Longest run from scrimmage in a single SB game
Marcus Allen, Raiders, 74TD
Marcus Allen, Raiders, 39
Highest average gain in a single SB game
Marcus Allen, Raiders, 9.5
Most passes attempted in a single SB game
Joe Theismann, Redskins, 35
Super Bowl XXV
Most rushing yards gained in a single SB game
Thurman Thomas, Bills, 135

Tampa Stadium, originally seating 47,000 fans, was built in 1967.

*A*vid Pirates fans attend a game at Pittsburgh's Three Rivers Stadium. Photo by Dave Arrigo, Pittsburgh Pirates

BASEBALL STADIUMS

Take Me Back to the Future

A funny thing happened to America's baseball parks on the way to the twenty-first century. In their race toward the future, they turned back the clock. Instead of continuing in the direction of retractable and fixed domes, symmetrical playing fields and artificial turf, modern ballparks are taking on a look that everyone thought went out with running boards and spats.

Following the lead of Baltimore's widely praised and wildly successful Oriole Park at Camden Yards, which has attracted more than 7 million fans since its inaugural game in 1992, major- and minor-league ball clubs and the cities, counties, and sports authorities that finance them are building a new generation of baseball-only parks with natural grass playing fields, asymmetrical dimensions, and ornate facades. Their smaller size (42,000-50,000 seats and generally smaller foul territory) places baseball spectators much closer to the field than the bowl-shaped multipurpose stadiums built in the sixties and seventies. Further, there is a growing tendency to use the new ballparks to anchor sports and cultural districts in urban neighborhoods that in earlier years housed factories, warehouses, and railroad yards.

Like country inns, in which wicker porch furniture and chintz curtains coexist with jacuzzis and computerized reservation systems, today's retro-genre ballparks are state-of-the-art, fan-friendly facilities that evoke yesteryear.

Take those green grandstand seats at Oriole Park at Camden Yards that look like the wooden ones your great-grandfather may have sat in when he wore a straw hat to the game in some forgotten ballpark on a Saturday afternoon. They're not wood; they're plastic molded to simulate wood. They're also wider and spaced to provide more leg room. Seats at Coors Field, also colored stadium green and modeled after the traditional wooden seats, boast higher backs and cup holders. (The Coors family, for whom the field is named, is, after all, in the beer business.) And Jacobs Field in Cleveland comes complete with a nineties version of the knothole; a window built into the fence at street level that permits passersby to catch a few

Above: Some stadiums, such as Cleveland's Jacobs Field, allow baseball fans who want more sophisticated fare than hot dogs and hamburgers to eat in on-site restaurants and still watch the game. Courtesy, HOK Sports Facilities Group

Right: This attractive and inviting restaurant is actually part of a minor-league ballpark— Buffalo's Pilot Field. Courtesy, HOK Sports Facilities Group

minutes of the game free.

The homey touches that have made stadium fans of baseball fans are also offset by thoroughly modern amenities such as luxury suites, food courts, kiddie parks, specially constructed and sited seating for disabled fans, interview rooms for the media, and indoor batting cages and pitching tunnels for players. Improvements carry over to the playing field; outfielders patrolling the grass-covered power alleys of the new parks are less likely to lose track of fly balls at night thanks to state-of-the-art field lighting.

Since Camden Yards opened in Baltimore in 1992, ballparks in its image have made their debut in Cleveland, with the Indians' 42,000-seat Jacobs Field (leaving the pro football Browns in sole possession of the cavernous Cleveland Stadium where Babe Ruth once complained he needed a horse to get around the outfield); in Arlington, Texas, with the Rangers' 48,000-seat The Ballpark at Arlington, built within sight of its predecessor, Arlington Stadium; and, with the 1995 season, the newly constructed 43,000-plus-seat Coors Field in downtown Denver, moving the Colorado Rockies out of Mile High Stadium and leaving it to the NFL's Denver Broncos.

With far less national fanfare, the new

Newly constructed Coors Field in downtown Denver seats 43,000 spectators for Colorado Rockies games. The structure's architectural style harkens back to an earlier era in stadium design. Courtesy, HOK Sports Facilities Group

44,000-seat Comiskey Park, where the Chicago White Sox play, opened in 1991 within a stone's throw of the site of its predecessor, the venerable old Comiskey Park. Lest anyone forget that Comiskey II, as it is now known, preceded Camden Yards by a year, the Chicago White Sox 1994 media guide takes pains to point out that the new stadium was the first major-league baseball-only facility to open since 1972, when Kansas City's Royals Stadium opened. (The honor of being the first new retro-genre ballpark goes to a minor-league stadium. Pilot Field, the downtown Buffalo, New York, home park of the Class AAA Bisons, opened for business in 1988.)

The next baseball-only facility in the majors is scheduled for Atlanta, where a 65,000-seat stadium being constructed for the 1996 Olympic Games will be converted to a 45,000-seat baseball park in time for the Braves' 1997 season. The Olympic stadium-turned-baseball park, whose brick facade will take its cues from historic Atlanta architecture, is to replace the adjacent Fulton County

Stadium scheduled for demolition at age 32 at the conclusion of the Olympics.

The current wave of major-league ballpark openings is only the opening inning in what promises to be a long series of stadium construction and renovation activity. The initial success of Oriole Park at Camden Yards and the other traditional urban ballparks, combined with the aging of the country's stadium stock, has major- and minor-league teams looking to build and upgrade their parks.

"By the end of the century, there will be a whole new generation of base-

ball parks, mainly for economic reasons," says Robert Bluthardt, chairman of the Ballparks Research Committee of the Society for American Baseball Research (SABR), a network of baseball enthusiasts and researchers. "A ballpark that's structurally obsolete is also financially obsolete. It's a worthwhile investment to tear down an older stadium and build a new one with plenty of luxury seating that can fetch up to $100,000 per season."

Part of that new generation of ballparks is being born in the minor leagues, populated by 230 teams from Class A to AAA. Once characterized by rickety wooden stands and chewing tobacco billboards, many minor-league parks have taken on the gloss of their big-league counterparts. Buffalo's Pilot Field and Charlotte Knights Baseball Stadium, built in 1990 for the AAA Charlotte (NC) Knights, offer the same amenities and diversions as big-league teams but with half the number of seats and at half the price.

One minor-league ballpark gives new meaning to the term *fan amenity.* Skysox Stadium (capacity 10,000), home of the AAA Colorado Springs Skysox, makes it possible for fans to watch games from a hot tub. Situated in the stands between first base and right field, the hot tub accommodates eight people. The rental price of $120 per game includes a bottle of champagne. Skysox officials report that there is already a waiting list for the 1996 season.

The Durham (NC) Bulls, a Class A affiliate of the Atlanta Braves, opened a new 7,000-seat ballpark in the traditional urban style in downtown Durham at the start of the 1995 season. The park was originally scheduled to be built in the Raleigh-Durham suburbs.

The stadium windfall is also spreading to

9t Could Only Happen In Brooklyn

Of all the bygone American ballparks, some of the fondest memories are reserved for Ebbets Field, home to the Brooklyn Dodgers from 1913 to 1960, when the club decamped for Los Angeles. When everyone from newspaper columnists to radio comics once observed that "it could only happen in Brooklyn," they were probably thinking of Ebbets Field, "Dem Bums," and their ardent fans. Where else would 500 fans, as they did one day in 1924, take down a telephone pole and use it as a battering ram to gain entry through the left field exit gate?

Ebbets Field was destined for eccentricity literally from the beginning. Read these words of Arthur Daley, whose columns once graced the sports pages of *The New York Times:*

Even the grand opening of Ebbets Field in 1913 was symptomatic of the entire operation. It was discovered that they had forgotten to build a press box. This discovery was slightly delayed because the varlet assigned to unlocking the gates had forgotten to bring the keys. But the big moment actually arrived, the grand march to the flagpole for the ceremony. No flag raising, though. They had forgotten the flag.

Brooklyn's Ebbets Field in the 1950s.

COURTESY, NATIONAL BASEBALL LIBRARY & ARCHIVE, COOPERSTOWN, N.Y., AND THE BROOKLYN MUSEUM

spring training facilities, as preseason baseball becomes more popular. Space Coast Stadium, the 7,500-seat preseason venue of the Florida Marlins in Melbourne, features $25,000 luxury suites and an 80-foot rocket outside the ballpark. The Yankees are building a 10,000-seat spring training stadium in Tampa, while the Red Sox now train in a new $22-million ballpark in Fort Myers. A $30-million spring training ballpark complex in the Phoenix, Arizona, suburb of Peoria is shared by the San Diego Padres and the Seattle Mariners.

Baseball fans, writers, historians, and preservationists agree that the motif that worked so well for Baltimore's Camden Yards and was packing fans into Jacobs Field and The Ballpark at Arlington is expected to build even greater interest in minor-league ball and is based on a simple premise: In baseball, as in no other spectator sport, fans prefer a stadium that is an integral part of the game and an eloquent expression of its traditions.

America's ballparks can claim almost as many fans as the teams and players they house. Names like Fenway, Wrigley, and Ebbets inspire an affection and reverence once reserved for names such as Williams, DiMaggio, and Musial. The Baseball Hall of Fame in Cooperstown, New York, is expanding its "ballparks room" by 30 percent to reflect this reverence. To even suggest that such icons as Boston's Fenway Park, Chicago's Wrigley Field, or Detroit's Tiger Stadium

Ballparks Ride the Winds of Change

A successful baseball park is built of brick, mortar, steel—and gamesmanship. Some say that the king of the gamesmen was the late Bill Veeck, Jr., who built a madcap reputation as owner of the Chicago White Sox. Veeck vexed opponents by, among other antics, putting an outfield fence on rollers so it could be moved out of slugger range, overwatering the base paths to slow down base runners, and befuddling visiting pitchers with soft spots on the pitcher's mound.

Bill Veeck may have passed on to the big ballpark in the sky, but stadium trickery lives on, notably in America's newer baseball parks. For example, both The Ballpark at Arlington and Jacobs Field in Cleveland hid the visitors' bullpens under the stands, giving relief pitchers and their coaches only a partial view of the field and their dugout.

The most sophisticated wrinkle, reported by *The Wall Street Journal* during the 1994 season, is wind control. Rowan, Williams, Davies & Irwin (RWDI), a Guelph, Ontario, laboratory specializing in wind currents, has been advising ballpark builders on how to position walls and other configurations to take maximum advantage of wind currents. By testing wind currents on plastic models of the ballparks, the laboratory could suggest construction alternatives to modulate winds, presumably in the home team's favor. RWDI's data, plugged into a computer along with information on pitchers and hitters and the readings from a wind gage, could be immeasurable help in planning pitching rotations and batting lineups. For example, the Texas Rangers redesigned portions of the outfield of The Ballpark at Arlington based on RWDI data to, some say, inhibit routine homers by opposing hitters while allowing big blasts by their own sluggers. And the Chicago White Sox used RWDI data in the design of the new Comiskey Park, an appropriate course of action for a team from the Windy City.

be replaced is to commit heresy of the gravest sort. In *Green Cathedrals,* a compendium of ballparks past and present, author Philip J. Lowry calls Wrigley Field "the most beautiful 4 acres of bluegrass in the world." Sometimes affection for a ballpark takes other forms. In the *Boston Red Sox Trivia Book,* novelist/Sox fan George V. Higgins writes, "Fenway was old when it was new. It is unsightly from the outside, looking like an old brick warehouse rambling around a misshapen plot of land." In Detroit thousands of members of the Tiger Stadium fan club "hugged" the ballpark by forming a human ring around its circumference to protest plans to tear it down. This outpouring of affection must have worked. Tiger Stadium is safe until 2008.

What is it about baseball parks that kindles such passion, loyalty, and nostalgia? Why don't other sports stadiums and arenas inspire similar fervor? Even the old Boston Garden, where the Celtics and Bruins built basketball and hockey dynasties, closed its doors amid few tears. There are almost as many explanations for this state of affairs as there are baseball fans.

"Baseball is connected intimately to the place in which it is played and derives much of its aura from that place," wrote cultural and architectural critic Paul Goldberger in *The New York Times.* "It is no accident that people do not merely like ballparks, they love them, and they remember them with passion."

"We tried to figure out why the people felt the way they did about the older ballparks, " says Texas Rangers' president Tom Schieffer of his decision to commission a neoclassic look for The Ballpark at Arlington. "We came away with the idea that the old ballparks had an intimacy between the fans and the players and between the community and the ballpark."

Quips Bob Bluthardt of the Society for American Baseball Research: "When a team plays 81 home games in the same park, fans

Facing page: With St. Louis' Gateway Arch always in view of Busch Stadium, the ballpark and the city are inextricably linked in the minds of baseball fans. Photo by James Blank / Scenics of America

Chicago's Wrigley Field, home of the Cubs, is an integral part of the surrounding neighborhood. Photo by James Blank / Scenics of America

have time to develop an intimacy."

"The ballpark is part of the game because the game interacts with the structure of the park," says Bill Goff, whose studio in Kent, Connecticut, has sold more than 30,000 limited-edition baseball prints, most of them renderings of old ballparks, since 1987. "Very often, the park, not the player, makes the play. How many times has a ball ricocheting around an outfield corner or taking a crazy hop on the infield dirt decided the outcome of a game? How often has a shot that would have been a homer in one park turn out to be just a long out in another?"

Ballparks play a special part in the lives of Americans. Truly obsessed baseball fans remember their first big-league ball game the way others remember their first love affair. Says the introduction of Houghton Mifflin's *The Ultimate Baseball Book*, "People have been born [in ballparks], gotten married in them, ritually taken their children to them, died in them, even had their remains scattered over them."

Political columnist/baseball writer George Will wrote in *Men at Work*, his

insightful book on what he calls the craft of baseball, "A fan remembers with special fondness where he saw his first major league game."

Philip J. Lowry writes: "For many, some special ballpark houses cherished childhood memories. For my grandfather, my father and me, that ballpark was [Pittsburgh's] Forbes Field."

Michael Gershman, author of *Diamonds: The Evolution of a Ballpark*, recalls accompanying his parents to Ebbets Field in Brooklyn at age 6. "I remember walking through the marble rotunda at the entrance, and how every sound echoed . . . and then I saw it—the grass on the field. It was like seeing Oz."

A. Bartlett Giamatti, who was baseball commissioner for only five months when he died in September 1989, apparently saw Oz in his own way. He was fond of noting that the root of the word "paradise" is an ancient Persian word meaning "enclosed park or green." He wrote: "Ballparks exist because there is in humanity a vestigial memory of an enclosed green space as a place of freedom or play."

▶ New York Yankees

Baseball became our national pastime by 1903 and in New York, a team

called the Highlanders took the field in the new American League.

Renamed the Yankees in 1913, that club would become one of the most

famous of all sports franchises. The legendary pinstripes first appeared

on the uniforms in 1915, and by 1921 the Yankees clinched the first of 33 American League pennants. Through baseball's first 125 years, many distinguishing marks can be found in the history of the Yankees. For many fans, the glories of this franchise have been benchmarks in their lives.

Over 100 million fans enjoy the memory of a ballgame played at Yankee Stadium. Opened in 1923, the stadium is as much a part of the legend as the game itself. The New York Yankees Baseball Complex in Tampa, Florida, will open in March 1996 and will serve as host for Major League Spring Training and Florida State League home games, as well as other sporting events and concerts. The stadium, modeled after Yankee Stadium, has a 10,000-seat capacity and will become a page in the memories of close to 400,000 visitors each year. Fans will easily recognize those "icons" familiar at Yankee Stadium, such as the frieze over the upper-deck seating bowl and the spelling out of the word "Yankees" as a graphic on the outside of the stadium.

The complex will house three baseball fields on 31 acres. Approaching the stadium, visitors will be

treated to a festive plaza located between the stadium and adjacent community use field. The community use field will host the home games of Hillsborough Community College. A formal court, also located on the plaza level, will serve as Monument Park with plaques honoring Yankee greats.

Source: *New York Yankees Yearbook*

The Yankee Baseball Complex in Tampa, Florida, will open in March 1996.

More than 100 million fans have attended games at New York's Yankee Stadium since 1923.

▶ Busch Stadium

In the late 1950s the 34 city blocks now occupied by Busch Stadium, home of the St. Louis Cardinals, were lifeless. Blighted buildings and dingy flophouses lined the streets. Downtown St. Louis was a dinosaur, meandering slowly, aimlessly, toward extinction. ❧ *Then came a*

Busch Stadium is the crown jewel of downtown St. Louis' redevelopment.

jewel that revitalized the city and pushed it toward modernization—Busch Stadium. In September 1959 the chamber of commerce approved a downtown redevelopment plan and the city's leading corporate citizen, Cardinals chairman August Busch, Jr., led the charge.

Anheuser-Busch contributed the first $5 million to the project as part of its extensive involvement. As a result, the stadium cost the city just $6 million—used to relocate streets and utilities. The return on that investment has been spectacular.

Busch Stadium has played host to five World Series games since its opening in 1966 and remains among the most attractive facilities in the country. Legendary moments and legendary names fill the stadium's history. In 1968 Hall of Famer Bob Gibson set a modern-day record with a 1.12 earned-run average and the Cardinals won another pennant.

In 1974 Lou Brock stole a Major League-record 118 bases. In 1977 Brock broke Ty Cobb's career mark for stolen bases and in 1979 he stroked his 3,000th hit at Busch, securing his place in Cooperstown.

The 1980s brought more glamour and glory. Anheuser-Busch, through subsidiary Civic Center Corp., purchased the stadium in 1981. Upon its acquisition, St. Louis benefited from Anheuser-Busch's ownership and commitment to quality, which resulted in innovations, stadium upgrades, and building cleanliness that helped to establish Busch Stadium as one of the country's finest entertainment facilities.

In 1985 the Cardinals stole a team

record 314 bases and met Kansas City in the "I-70 Series." In 1987 attendance eclipsed 3 million. All along, spectators thrilled to the acrobatics of shortstop Ozzie Smith. The future Hall of Famer continues to be a fixture for the Cardinals and the community in the 1990s.

But baseball is just a sliver of the history and pageantry of Busch Stadium. Versatility has been one of its most endearing qualities. On August 21, 1966, the Beatles came to Busch. Despite a rainy evening, more than 23,000 came to see the Fab Four and some 35 girls were treated for "mild hysteria."

During the 1990s Busch Stadium, the crown jewel of downtown St. Louis' redevelopment, has become an increasingly integral part of the community, hosting a variety of sports, entertainment, and charity events.

Outside the stadium, on the "Plaza of Champions," stands a statue of Stan "The Man" Musial along with monuments dedicated to the club's nine World Championship teams. The inscription on the Musial statue, attributed to Ford Frick, reads: "Here Stands Baseball's Perfect Warrior: Here Stands Baseball's Perfect Knight."

The statue has become a landmark and a fitting ornament to the style and substance of Busch Stadium. For so many, it is baseball's perfect stadium.

The stadium has played host to five World Series since its opening in 1966.